The Round

Reigen

Arthur Schnitzler

An English-German Dual-Language Book
English Translation by Marya Mannes

Omo Press

adolescentium alunt
senectutem oblectant

ISBN: 978-1-941667-08-8

The cover is based on the cover of the original 1903 publication by Wiener Verlag

Note on the translation:

The title *Reigen* and its French translation, *La Ronde*, are both the names of dances done in a round.

The English translation by Marya Mannes was originally published under the title *Hands Around*, which readers at the time would have recognized as the name of a circle dance.

We have changed the name to *The Round*, because today's readers would not recognize "hands around" as the name of a dance and because The Round is similar to the well-known French title, *La Ronde*.

Apart from the title, we have not changed this 1917 translation, though it occasionally uses old-fashioned expressions, such as "tart" for "prostitute."

Reigen

Zehn Dialoge

Arthur Schnitzler

The Round

Ten Dialogs

Arthur Schnitzler

Inhalt

Contents

1: Die Dirne und der Soldat

Spät Abends. An der Augartenbrücke. Soldat kommt pfeifend, will nach Hause

Dirne: Komm, mein schöner Engel. [Soldat wendet sich um und geht wieder weiter.] Willst du nicht mit mir kommen?

Soldat: Ah, ich bin der schöne Engel?

Dirne: Freilich, wer denn? Geh', komm' zu mir. Ich wohn' gleich in der Näh'.

Soldat: Ich hab' keine Zeit. Ich muß in die Kasern'!

Dirne: In die Kasern' kommst immer noch zurecht. Bei mir is besser.

Soldat: [ihr nahe.] Das ist schon möglich.

Dirne: Pst. Jeden Moment kann ein Wachmann kommen.

Soldat: Lächerlich! Wachmann! Ich hab' auch mein Seiteng'wehr!

Dirne: Geh', komm' mit.

Soldat: Laß mich in Ruh'. Geld hab' ich eh kein's.

Dirne: Ich brauch' kein Geld.

Soldat: [bleibt stehen. Sie sind bei einer Laterne.] Du brauchst kein Geld? Wer bist denn du nachher?

Dirne: Zahlen tun mir die Zivilisten. So einer wie du, kann's immer umsonst bei mir haben.

Soldat: Du bist am End' die, von der mir der Huber erzählt hat. —

Dirne: Ich kenn' kein' Huber nicht.

Soldat: Du wirst schon die sein. Weißt — in dem Kaffeehaus in der Schiffgassen — von dort ist er mit dir z' Haus gangen.

Dirne: Von dem Kaffeehaus bin ich schon mit gar vielen z' Haus gangen ... oh! oh! —

Soldat: Also geh'n wir, geh'n wir.

1: The Tart and the Soldier

Late evening. A bridge over the Danube. The soldier enters whistling, on his way back to the barracks.

Tart: Come on, dearie. [The soldier turns around but proceeds on his way.] Come on, won't you?

Soldier: Oh, so I'm dearie?

Tart: Sure, who else? Come on with me, why don't you? I live right near.

Soldier: Got no time. Got to get back to the barracks.

Tart: Oh you'll get back to the barracks alright. My place is lots nicer.

Soldier: [Close to her.] Maybe so.

Tart: Pst. A policeman might come any moment.

Soldier: You're crazy! Policeman! I've got my bayonet, haven't I?

Tart: Aw, come on, won't you?

Soldier: Leave me alone. I got no money.

Tart: I don't need your money.

Soldier: [Standing still, they are under a street lamp.] You don't need money? Who do you think you are, anyway?

Tart: Oh I get money from the civilians. But a fellow like you can get it free, any time.

Soldier: I guess you're the one my pal Huber told me about —

Tart: Don't know any Huber.

Soldier: You're the one, alright. He picked you up in that Café down by the river and went home with you.

Tart: Lord, I've gone home with plenty from that Café, dearie!

Soldier: Well, come on, let's go.

Dirne: Was, jetzt hast's eilig?

Soldat: Na, worauf soll'n wir noch warten? Und um Zehn muß ich in der Kasern' sein.

Dirne: Wie lang dienst denn schon?

Soldat: Was geht denn das dich an? Wohnst weit?

Dirne: Zehn Minuten zum geh'n.

Soldat: Das ist mir zu weit. Gib mir ein Pussel.

Dirne: [küßt ihn.] Das ist mir eh das liebste, wenn ich einen gern' hab'!

Soldat: Mir nicht. Nein, ich geh' nicht mit dir, es ist mir zu weit.

Dirne: Weißt was, komm' morgen am Nachmittag.

Soldat: Gut is. Gib mir deine Adresse.

Dirne: Aber du kommst am End' nicht.

Soldat: Wenn ich dir's sag'!

Dirne: Du, weißt was — wenn's dir zu weit ist heut' Abend zu mir — da ... da ... [weist auf die Donau.]

Soldat: Was ist das?

Dirne: Da ist auch schön ruhig ... jetzt kommt kein Mensch.

Soldat: Ah, das ist nicht das rechte.

Dirne: Bei mir is immer das rechte. Geh', bleib' jetzt bei mir. Wer weiß, ob wir morgen noch 's Leben haben.

Soldat: So komm' — aber g'schwind!

Dirne: Gib obacht, da ist so dunkel. Wennst ausrutsch'st, liegst in der Donau.

Soldat: Wär' eh das Beste.

Dirne: Pst, so wart' nur ein bissel. Gleich kommen wir zu einer Bank.

Soldat: Kennst dich da gut aus.

Dirne: So einen wie dich möcht' ich zum Geliebten.

Soldat: Ich tät' dir zu viel eifern.

Dirne: Das möcht' ich dir schon abgewöhnen.

Soldat: Ha —

Dirne: Nicht so laut. Manchmal is doch, daß sich ein Wachter her verirrt. Sollt man glauben, daß wir da mitten in der Wienerstadt sind?

Soldat: Daher komm', daher.

Tart: What's your hurry now?

Soldier: Well, what's the use of waitin'? I got to be in the barracks by ten.

Tart: Been in the service long?

Soldier: What's that got to do with you? How far do you live?

Tart: Ten minutes walk.

Soldier: That's too far for me. Gimme a kiss.

Tart: [Kissing him.] Suits me fine when I like a fellow!

Soldier: Well, it don't suit me. No, I'm not goin' with you, it's too damn far.

Tart: I know what, come tomorrow afternoon, huh?

Soldier: Good idea. Gimme your address.

Tart: But you won't turn up, I know your kind.

Soldier: Listen, you can count on me!

Tart: See here — if it's too far for you to come home tonight, how about down there — [Points toward the Danube.]

Soldier: What's down there?

Tart: It's nice and quiet there ... no one'll come around.

Soldier: Oh, that's not the real thing.

Tart: It's always the real thing with me, sweetie. Aw, come on, stay with me. Tomorrow maybe we're dead!

Soldier: Alright then, but make it fast.

Tart: Look out, though, it's pitch black down there. If you slip you'll land in the Danube.

Soldier: Might be the best thing.

Tart: Pst, go easy now. We're almost at the bench.

Soldier: You know your way around alright.

Tart: I'd like a fellow like you for a sweetheart.

Soldier: I'd keep you too damn busy!

Tart: I'd put a stop to that soon enough.

Soldier: That's a good one! Ha!

Tart: Quiet, will you? Once in a while a watchman does stumble into this place. God, would you believe we was right in the middle of the city?

Soldier: Come on, here —

Dirne: Aber was fällt dir denn ein, wenn wir da ausrutschen, liegen wir im Wasser unten.

Soldat: [hat sie gepackt.] Ah, du —

Dirne: Halt dich nur fest an.

Soldat: Hab kein' Angst ....

* * * * *

Dirne: Auf der Bank wär's schon besser gewesen.

Soldat: Da oder da .... Na, krall' aufi.

Dirne: Was laufst denn so —

Soldat: Ich muß in die Kasern', ich komm' eh schon zu spät.

Dirne: Geh', du, wie heißt denn?

Soldat: Was interessiert dich denn das, wie ich heiß?

Dirne: Ich heiß Leocadia.

Soldat: Ha! — So an' Namen hab' ich auch noch nie gehört.

Dirne: Du!

Soldat: Na, was willst denn?

Dirne: Geh, ein Sechserl für'n Hausmeister gib mir wenigstens! —

Soldat: Ha!... Glaubst, ich bin deine Wurzen ... Servus! Leocadia ...

Dirne: Strizzi! Fallott! —

[Er ist verschwunden..]

Tart: You're crazy, if we slip we'll roll right down in the water.

Soldier: [Seizing her.] Oh, you —

Tart: Hold on tight.

Soldier: Don't worry ...

* * * * *

Tart: We should've gone to the bench.

Soldier: Aw, who cares? ... Well, get a move on, will you?

Tart: What's your hurry?

Soldier: I got to get back to the barracks, I'm late already.

Tart: What's your name, anyway?

Soldier: What's my name got to do with you?

Tart: My name's Leocadia.

Soldier: Ha! That's the first time I've banged a name like that.

Tart: Say —

Soldier: What do you want now?

Tart: You might slip me a bit for carfare, at least!

Soldier: Ha! ... Take me for a sucker? ... So long, Leocadia!

Tart: Bum! Piker!
[He has disappeared.]

2: Der Soldat und das Stubenmädchen

Prater. Sonntag Abend. Ein Weg, der vom Wurstelprater aus in die dunkeln Alleen führt. Hier hört man noch die wirre Musik aus dem Wurstelprater; auch die Klänge vom Fünfkreuzertanz, eine ordinäre Polka, von Bläsern gespielt.

Stubenmädchen: Jetzt sagen S' mir aber, warum S' durchaus schon haben fortgehen müssen. [Soldat lacht verlegen, dumm.] Es ist doch so schön gewesen. Ich tanz' so gern'. [Soldat faßt sie um die Taille. Stubenmädchen läßt's geschehen.] Jetzt tanzen wir ja nimmer. Warum halten S' mich so fest?

Soldat: Wie heißen S'? Kathi?

Stubenmädchen: Ihnen ist immer eine Kathi im Kopf.

Soldat: Ich weiß, ich weiß schon .... Marie.

Stubenmädchen: Sie, da ist aber dunkel. Ich krieg' so eine Angst.

Soldat: Wenn ich bei Ihnen bin, brauchen S' Ihnen nicht zu fürchten. Gott sei Dank, mir sein mir!

Stubenmädchen: Aber wohin kommen wir denn da? Da ist ja kein Mensch mehr. Kommen S', gehn wir zurück! — Und so dunkel!

Soldat: [zieht an seiner Virginierzigarre, daß das rote Ende leuchtet.] 's wird schon lichter! Haha! O, du Schatzerl!

Stubenmädchen: Ah, was machen S' denn? Wenn ich das gewußt hätt'!

Soldat: Also der Teufel soll mich holen, wenn eine heut' beim Swoboda mollerter gewesen ist als Sie, Fräul'n Marie.

Stubenmädchen: Haben S' denn bei allen so probiert?

Soldat: Was man so merkt, beim Tanzen. Da merkt man gar viel! Ha!

2: The Soldier and the Chambermaid

The Prater. Sunday Night. A path leading from the Amusement Park to the dark lanes. One can still hear the confused and jangling music from the Amusement Park, and the trombone strains of an ordinary Polka.

Chambermaid: Come on, now, tell me why you had to leave so soon, anyway. [Soldier laughs stupidly, in embarrassment.] It was so lovely there. I'm crazy about dancing. [Soldier grabs her around the waist. She does not protest.] We're not dancing anymore. What are you holding me so tight for?

Soldier: What's your name? Kathi?

Chambermaid: You've always got a Kathi on the brain.

Soldier: Oh I know what it is ... Marie.

Chambermaid: Lordy, it's dark here. It kinda scares me.

Soldier: You needn't be scared when you're with me. Thank God I'm the man I am!

Chambermaid: But where are we heading for, anyway? There ain't a soul here. Please, let's go on back! Lord, it's dark!

Soldier: [Drawing on his cigar so that the end glows red.] It's gettin' lighter now. Ha ha! Oh you sweetie, you!

Chambermaid: Hey, what are you doin'? If I'd a known —!

Soldier: I'll be damned if there was a plumper piece of goods in the dance-hall than you, Miss Marie.

Chambermaid: Did you try 'em all out?

Soldier: Oh you can find out plenty just dancing. And how! Crikey!

Stubenmädchen: Aber mit der blonden mit dem schiefen Gesicht haben S' doch mehr 'tanzt als mit mir.

Soldat: Das ist eine alte Bekannte von einem meinigen Freund.

Stubenmädchen: Von dem Korporal mit dem auf'drehten Schnurrbart?

Soldat: Ah nein, das ist der Zivilist gewesen, wissen S', der im Anfang am Tisch mit mir g'sessen ist, der so heis'rig red't.

Stubenmädchen: Ah, ich weiß schon. Das ist ein kecker Mensch.

Soldat: Hat er Ihnen was 'tan? Dem möcht' ich's zeigen! Was hat er Ihnen 'tan?

Stubenmädchen: Oh nichts — ich hab nur geseh'n, wie er mit die andern ist.

Soldat: Sagen S', Fräulein Marie ....

Stubenmädchen: Sie werden mich verbrennen mit Ihrer Zigarrn.

Soldat: Pahdon! — Fräul'n Marie. Sagen wir uns Du.

Stubenmädchen: Wir sein noch nicht so gute Bekannte. —

Soldat: Es können sich gar viele nicht leiden und sagen doch Du zueinander.

Stubenmädchen: 's nächstemal, wenn wir ... Aber, Herr Franz —

Soldat: Sie haben sich meinen Namen g'merkt?

Stubenmädchen: Aber, Herr Franz ....

Soldat: Sagen S' Franz, Fräulein Marie.

Stubenmädchen: So sein S' nicht so keck — aber pst, wenn wer kommen tät!

Soldat: Und wenn schon einer kommen tät, man sieht ja nicht zwei Schritt weit.

Stubenmädchen: Aber um Gotteswillen, wohin kommen wir denn da?

Soldat: Sehn S', da sind zwei g'rad wie mir.

Stubenmädchen: Wo denn? Ich seh' gar nichts.

Soldat: Da ... vor uns.

Stubenmädchen: Warum sagen S' denn: zwei wie mir? —

Chambermaid: But you did dance more with that crooked-faced blonde than you did with me.

Soldier: She's an old friend of an old friend of mine.

Chambermaid: That corporal with the turned-up moustache!

Soldier: Oh no, the civilian, you know, the man who sat at the table with me at first, with the beery voice.

Chambermaid: Oh sure, I know. That's a fresh feller, that is.

Soldier: Did he get fresh with you? Wait till I get at him. What did he do to you?

Chambermaid: Oh nothing — I just saw how he was with the others.

Soldier: Listen, Miss Marie ...

Chambermaid: You'll burn me with that cigar.

Soldier: Beg your pardon — Miss Marie. Say, how about gettin' a little chummy, eh?

Chambermaid: I don't know you very well yet ...

Soldier: Hell, lots of people get chummy before they know each other.

Chambermaid: Well, perhaps, next time when we ... But Mr. Franz —

Soldier: So you've found out my name, have you?

Chambermaid: But Mr. Franz —

Soldier: Leave off the Mister, Marie.

Chambermaid: Say, don't be so fresh — what if somebody came!

Soldier: What if they did, you can't see a damn thing here.

Chambermaid: For goodness sakes, what do you think you're doing, anyway?

Soldier: Look, there's two just like us.

Chambermaid: Where? I don't see anything.

Soldier: There — in front of us.

Chambermaid: What do you mean — "just like us"?

Soldat: Na, ich mein' halt, die haben sich auch gern'.

Stubenmädchen: Aber geben S' doch acht, was ist denn da, jetzt wär' ich beinah' g'fallen.

Soldat: Ah, das ist das Gatter von der Wiesen.

Stubenmädchen: Stoßen S' doch nicht so, ich fall' ja um.

Soldat: Pst, nicht so laut.

Stubenmädchen: Sie, jetzt schrei ich aber wirklich. — Aber was machen S' denn ... aber —

Soldat: Da ist jetzt weit und breit keine Seel'.

Stubenmädchen: So gehn wir zurück, wo Leut sein.

Soldat: Wir brauchen keine Leut, was, Marie, wir brauchen .... dazu .... haha.

Stubenmädchen: Aber, Herr Franz, bitt' Sie, um Gotteswillen, schaun S', wenn ich das .... gewußt .... oh .... oh .... komm!....

Soldat: [selig.] Herrgott noch einmal .... ah ....

Stubenmädchen: .... Ich kann dein G'sicht gar nicht sehn.

Soldat: A was — G'sicht .....

* * * * *

Soldat: Ja, Sie, Fräul'n Marie, da im Gras können S' nicht liegen bleiben.

Stubenmädchen: Geh', Franz, hilf mir.

Soldat: Na, komm zugi.

Stubenmädchen: Oh Gott, Franz.

Soldat: Na ja, was ist denn mit dem Franz?

Stubenmädchen: Du bist ein schlechter Mensch, Franz.

Soldat: Ja, ja. Geh', wart' ein bissel.

Stubenmädchen: Was laßt mich denn aus?

Soldat: Na, die Virginier werd' ich mir doch anzünden dürfen.

Stubenmädchen: Es ist so dunkel.

Soldat: Morgen früh ist schon wieder licht.

Stubenmädchen: Sag' wenigstens, hast mich gern'?

Soldat: Na, das mußt doch g'spürt haben, Fräul'n Marie, ha!

Stubenmädchen: Wohin geh'n wir denn?

Soldat: Na, zurück.

Stubenmädchen: Geh', bitt' dich, nicht so schnell!

Soldat: Na, was ist denn? Ich geh' nicht gern' in der finstern.

Soldier: Oh well, I mean, they like each other too.
Chambermaid: Say, look out, will you? I almost fell.

Soldier: Oh, that's the fence, I guess.
Chambermaid: If you keep on pushing like that I'll fall down.
Soldier: Ssshh, not so loud.
Chambermaid: I'll scream if you don't look out — See here, what are you doin' — say —
Soldier: There isn't a soul anywheres near.
Chambermaid: Let's go on back where there are people.
Soldier: We don't need people, do we, baby, to ... Ha ha.

Chambermaid: But for God's sakes, Mr. Franz, honest — if I'd a known — Oh my God — look out — Oh —!

Soldier: [Blissfully.] Lord almighty! ... Oh! ...
Chambermaid: ... I can't see your face at all.
Soldier: Face, hell ...

* * * * *

Soldier: Look here, Marie, you can't just lay there on the grass all night.
Chambermaid: Well, help me up then.
Soldier: Up you go, baby.
Chambermaid: Oh my God, Franz.
Soldier: What's the matter now?
Chambermaid: You're a bad lot, Franz.
Soldier: Sure, sure. Hey, wait a minute.
Chambermaid: You're not going to leave me here!
Soldier: Let a fellow light a cigarette, can't you?
Chambermaid: It's awful dark.
Soldier: It'll be light again tomorrow morning.
Chambermaid: Say you like me a little, don't you?
Soldier: Lord, you must have felt I did, Marie!
Chambermaid: Where are we going now?
Soldier: Back, of course.
Chambermaid: Don't walk so fast!
Soldier: What's worrying you? I don't like walking in the dark.

Stubenmädchen: Sag', Franz, hast mich gern'?

Soldat: Aber grad' hab' ich's g'sagt, daß ich dich gern' hab'!

Stubenmädchen: Geh', willst mir nicht ein Pussel geben?

Soldat: [gnädig.] Da .... Hörst, — jetzt kann man schon wieder die Musik hören.

Stubenmädchen: Du möcht'st am End' gar wieder tanzen geh'n?

Soldat: Na freilich, was denn?

Stubenmädchen: Ja, Franz, schau, ich muß zu Haus geh'n. Sie werden eh schon schimpfen, mei' Frau ist so eine .... die möcht' am liebsten, man ging gar nicht fort.

Soldat: Na ja, geh' halt zu Haus.

Stubenmädchen: Ich hab' halt 'dacht, Herr Franz, Sie werden mich z'hausführen.

Soldat: Z'hausführen? Ah!

Stubenmädchen: Geh'n S', es ist so traurig, allein z'haus geh'n.

Soldat: Wo wohnen S' denn?

Stubenmädchen: Es ist gar nicht so weit — in der Porzellangasse.

Soldat: So? Ja, da haben wir ja einen Weg .... aber jetzt ist's mir zu früh ... jetzt wird noch 'draht, heut hab' ich über Zeit ..... vor zwölf brauch' ich nicht in der Kasern' zu sein. I' geh' noch tanzen.

Stubenmädchen: Freilich, ich weiß schon, jetzt kommt die Blonde mit dem schiefen Gesicht d'ran!

Soldat: Ha! — Der ihr G'sicht ist gar nicht so schief.

Stubenmädchen: Oh Gott, sein die Männer schlecht. Was, Sie machen's sicher mit einer jeden so.

Soldat: Das wär' z'viel! —

Stubenmädchen: Franz, bitt' schön, heut' nimmer, — heut' bleiben S' mit mir, schaun S' —

Soldat: Ja, ja, ist schon gut. Aber tanzen werd' ich doch noch dürfen.

Stubenmädchen: Ich tanz' heut' mit kein' mehr!

Soldat: Da ist er ja schon ..

Stubenmädchen: Wer denn?

Soldat: Der Swoboda! Wie schnell wir wieder da sein. Noch immer spielen s' das ... tadarada tadarada [singt mit.]

Chambermaid: Say, do you like me a little, Franz?

Soldier: I just told you I did, didn't I?

Chambermaid: Come on, give me a kiss, huh?

Soldier: [Condescendingly.] There ... Listen — you can hear the music again.

Chambermaid: I suppose you want to dance again?

Soldier: Sure, why not?

Chambermaid: Well, you see, Franz, I've got to go home. They'll be sore at me already, my missus don't like me to go out at all, anyhow.

Soldier: Alright then, run along home.

Chambermaid: I kinda thought you'd take me home, Mr. Franz.

Soldier: Take you home? Oh —

Chambermaid: It's sorta lonesome goin' home all alone —

Soldier: Where do you live, anyway?

Chambermaid: It ain't far at all — it's in Porzellan Street.

Soldier: That so? Well, that's pretty much on my way ... but it's too early for me now ... it's my night out, I don't have to be back at the barracks before twelve. I'm goin' to dance some more.

Chambermaid: Oh I know you, now it's the pie-faced blonde's turn!

Soldier: Ha! She's not so damn pie-faced at that.

Chambermaid: Oh God, men are awful. I bet you treat 'em all like this.

Soldier: All's a bit too much!

Chambermaid: Please, Franz — just for tonight — stay with me, won't you —?

Soldier: Alright, alright. But I can have a few more dances, can't I?

Chambermaid: I ain't goin' to dance with no one no more!

Soldier: Here we are already ...

Chambermaid: Where?

Soldier: Back at the dance-hall, of course! How quick we got back. They're still playing that ... tadatara tadatara —

.... Also wannst auf mich warten willst, so führ' ich dich z'haus .... wenn nicht ... Servas —

Stubenmädchen: Ja, ich werd' warten.

[Sie treten in den Tanzsaal ein.]

Soldat: Wissen S', Fräul'n Marie, ein Glas Bier lassen's Ihnen geben [Zu einer Blonden sich wendend, die eben mit einem Burschen vorbeitanzt, sehr hochdeutsch.] Mein Fräulein, darf ich bitten? —

[Sings.] Well then, if you want to wait for me I'll take you home ... if you don't ... tootly-oo —

Chambermaid: I'll wait for you.

[They step into the dance hall.]

Soldier: Treat yourself to a glass of beer, Miss Marie. [Turning to a blonde girl who is just dancing with a youth, very politely.] May I have a dance, Miss? —

3: Das Stubenmädchen und der junge Herr

Heißer Sommernachmittag. Die Eltern sind schon auf dem Lande. Die Köchin hat Ausgang. Das Stubenmädchen schreibt in der Küche einen Brief an den Soldaten, der ihr Geliebter ist. Es klingelt aus dem Zimmer des jungen Herrn. Sie steht auf und geht ins Zimmer des jungen Herrn.

Der junge Herr liegt auf dem Divan, raucht, und liest einen französischen Roman.

Das Stubenmädchen: Bitt' schön, junger Herr?

Der junge Herr: Ah ja, Marie, ah ja, ich hab' geläutet, ja ... was hab' ich nur ... ja richtig, die Rouletten lassen S' herunter, Marie ... Es ist kühler, wenn die Rouletten unten sind .... ja .... [Das Stubenmädchen geht zum Fenster und läßt die Rouletten herunter.]

Der junge Herr: [liest weiter.] Was machen S' denn, Marie? Ah ja. Jetzt sieht man aber gar nichts zum Lesen.

Das Stubenmädchen: Der junge Herr ist halt immer so fleißig.

Der junge Herr: [überhört das vornehm.] So, ist gut.

[Marie geht. Der junge Herr versucht weiter zu lesen; läßt bald das Buch fallen, klingelt wieder. Das Stubenmädchen erscheint.]

Der junge Herr: Sie, Marie .... ja, was ich habe sagen wollen .... ja .... ist vielleicht ein Cognac zu Haus?

Das Stubenmädchen: Ja, der wird eingesperrt sein.

Der junge Herr: Na, wer hat denn die Schlüssel?

Das Stubenmädchen: Die Schlüssel hat die Lini.

Der junge Herr: Wer ist die Lini?

Das Stubenmädchen: Die Köchin, Herr Alfred.

Der junge Herr: Na, so sagen S' es halt der Lini.

Das Stubenmädchen: Ja, die Lini hat heut Ausgang.

3: The Chambermaid and the Young Gentleman

A hot summer's afternoon. The parents have already gone to the country. It is the cook's day off. In the kitchen the chambermaid is writing a letter to her soldier sweetheart. The bell rings from the Young gentleman's room. She rises and goes to his room.

The young gentleman is lying on the sofa, smoking and reading a French novel.

Chambermaid: Pardon me, sir, did you ring?

Young Gentleman: Oh yes, Marie, Oh yes, I guess I did ring, didn't I? ... Now what was it I wanted ... Ah yes, of course, the blinds ... let down the blinds, Marie ... It's much cooler when the blinds are down ... [Chambermaid goes to window and lets down the blinds.]

Young gentleman: [starts reading again.] What are you doing, Marie? Oh yes. But it's too dark to read now ...

Chambermaid: You're always so busy studying, sir.

Young Gentleman: [Loftily.] Yes ... yes ...

[Marie goes. Young gentleman tries to read further, but soon lets the book fall and rings again. Chambermaid appears.]

Young Gentleman: By the way, Marie ... now, what was I going to say ... Oh yes, is there any Cognac in the house?

Chambermaid: Yes, sir, but it's locked up, I guess.

Young Gentleman: Well, who has the keys?

Chambermaid: Lini has them.

Young Gentleman: Who's Lini?

Chambermaid: She's the cook, Mr. Alfred.

Young Gentleman: Well, go and tell Lini.

Chambermaid: It's her day off, sir.

Der junge Herr: So .....

Das Stubenmädchen: Soll ich dem jungen Herrn vielleicht aus dem Kaffeehaus ....

Der junge Herr: Ah nein .... es ist so heiß genug. Ich brauch keinen Cognac. Wissen S', Marie, bringen Sie mir ein Glas Wasser. Pst, Marie — aber laufen lassen, daß es recht kalt ist.

[Das Stubenmädchen ab. Der junge Herr sieht ihr nach, bei der Thür wendet sich das Stubenmädchen nach ihm um; der junge Herr schaut in die Luft. — Das Stubenmädchen dreht den Hahn der Wasserleitung auf, läßt das Wasser laufen. Während dem geht sie in ihr kleines Kabinett, wäscht sich die Hände, richtet vor dem Spiegel ihre Schneckerln. Dann bringt sie dem jungen Herrn das Glas Wasser. Sie tritt zum Divan. Der junge Herr richtet sich zur Hälfte auf, das Stubenmädchen gibt ihm das Glas in die Hand, ihre Finger berühren sich.]

Der junge Herr: So, danke. — Na, was ist denn? — Geben Sie acht; stellen Sie das Glas wieder auf die Tasse .... [Er legt sich hin und streckt sich aus.] Wie spät ist's denn?

Das Stubenmädchen: Fünf Uhr, junger Herr.

Der junge Herr: So, fünf Uhr. — Ist gut. —

[Das Stubenmädchen geht; bei der Tür wendet sie sich um; der junge Herr hat ihr nachgeschaut; sie merkt es und lächelt. Der junge Herr bleibt eine Weile liegen, dann steht er plötzlich auf. Er geht bis zur Tür, wieder zurück, legt sich auf den Divan. Er versucht wieder zu lesen. Nach ein paar Minuten klingelt er wieder. Das Stubenmädchen erscheint mit einem Lächeln, das sie nicht zu verbergen sucht.]

Der junge Herr: Sie, Marie, was ich Sie hab' fragen wollen. War heut' Vormittag nicht der Doktor Schüller da?

Das Stubenmädchen: Nein, heut Vormittag war niemand da.

Der junge Herr: So, das ist merkwürdig. Also der Doktor Schüller war nicht da? Kennen Sie überhaupt den Doktor Schüller?

Das Stubenmädchen: Freilich. Das ist der große Herr mit dem schwarzen Vollbart.

Young Gentleman: Oh —

Chambermaid: Shall I go get some from the Café, sir?

Young Gentleman: No, don't bother ... it's hot enough as it is. I don't need any Cognac. You might bring me a glass of water, though, Marie. But wait ... let it run till it's good and cold.

[Chambermaid goes out. Young gentleman looks at her. As she reaches the door, she turns around and looks at him. He promptly gazes into the air. The Chambermaid turns on the water faucet, letting it run. Then she goes into her small room, washes her hands, tidies her hair in front of the mirror. Then she brings the glass of water to the Young gentleman, approaching the sofa as she does so. The Young gentleman half raises himself from the sofa, the Chambermaid hands him the glass, and their fingers touch.]

Young Gentleman: Thanks. What's the matter? Be careful, put the glass back on the tray ... [He lies down again and stretches himself full length.] What time is it, anyway?

Chambermaid: Five o'clock, sir.

Young Gentleman: Oh, five ... Alright.

[Chambermaid goes, turns around as she reaches the door and smiles as she notices that the Young gentleman has watched her. The Young gentleman remains lying down for a while, then suddenly stands up. He walks to the door then back again and lies down on the sofa. Tries to read again. After a few moments, he rings again. Chambermaid appears, with a smile that she does not attempt to conceal.]

Young Gentleman: By the way, Marie, I've been wanting to ask you — wasn't Doctor Schueller here this morning?

Chambermaid: No, nobody was here this morning.

Young Gentleman: That's strange. Doctor Schueller wasn't here at all? Do you know Doctor Schueller anyway?

Chambermaid: Sure I do. He's the tall gentleman with the black beard.

Der junge Herr: Ja. War er vielleicht doch da?

Das Stubenmädchen: Nein, es war niemand da, junger Herr.

Der junge Herr: [entschlossen.] Kommen Sie her, Marie.

Das Stubenmädchen [tritt etwas näher.]. Bitt' schön.

Der junge Herr: Näher .... so .... ah .... ich hab' nur geglaubt .....

Das Stubenmädchen: Was haben der junge Herr?

Der junge Herr: Geglaubt .... geglaubt hab' ich — Nur wegen Ihrer Blusen .... Was ist das für eine .... Na, kommen S' nur näher. Ich beiß Sie ja nicht.

Das Stubenmädchen: [kommt zu ihm.] Was ist mit meiner Blusen? G'fallt sie dem jungen Herrn nicht?

Der junge Herr: [faßt die Bluse an, wobei er das Stubenmädchen zu sich herabzieht.] Blau? Das ist ganz ein schönes Blau. [Einfach.] Sie sind sehr nett angezogen, Marie.

Das Stubenmädchen: Aber junger Herr ....

Der junge Herr: Na, was ist denn?.... [er hat ihre Bluse geöffnet. Sachlich.] Sie haben eine schöne weiße Haut, Marie.

Das Stubenmädchen: Der junge Herr tut mir schmeicheln.

Der junge Herr: [küßt sie auf die Brust.] Das kann doch nicht weh' tun.

Das Stubenmädchen: O nein.

Der junge Herr: Weil Sie so seufzen! Warum seufzen Sie denn?

Das Stubenmädchen: Oh, Herr Alfred ....

Der junge Herr: Und was Sie für nette Pantoffeln haben ....

Das Stubenmädchen: .... Aber .... junger Herr .... wenn's draußen läut' —

Der junge Herr: Wer wird denn jetzt läuten?

Das Stubenmädchen: Aber junger Herr .... schaun S' .... es ist so licht ....

Der junge Herr: Vor mir brauchen Sie sich nicht zu genieren. Sie brauchen sich überhaupt vor niemandem .... wenn man so hübsch ist. Ja, meiner Seel'; Marie, Sie sind .... Wissen Sie, Ihre Haare riechen sogar angenehm.

Das Stubenmädchen: Herr Alfred ....

Der junge Herr: Machen Sie keine solchen Geschichten,

Young Gentleman: Yes. You're sure he wasn't here, after all?

Chambermaid: No, sir, nobody was here.

Young Gentleman: [With decision.] Come here, Marie.

Chambermaid: [Coming nearer.] Yes, sir.

Young Gentleman: Closer ... that's right ... I was just wondering ...

Chambermaid: What were you wondering, sir?

Young Gentleman: Wondering ... wondering — about your blouse ... what kind of material ... come on, come a little closer. I won't bite you.

Chambermaid: [Coming closer.] What about my blouse? Don't you like it, sir?

Young Gentleman: [Touching the blouse and drawing her towards him.] Blue ... and a very lovely blue. [Simply.] You dress very nicely, Marie.

Chambermaid: But, sir ...

Young Gentleman: Well, what's the matter? ... [Opens her blouse. Matter of fact.] You have a beautiful white skin, Marie.

Chambermaid: You're flattering me, sir.

Young Gentleman: [Kissing her breast.] That can't hurt you.

Chambermaid: Oh no.

Young Gentleman: You sigh so. What are you sighing for?

Chambermaid: Oh, Mr. Alfred ...

Young Gentleman: What pretty slippers you have on ...

Chambermaid: But ... sir ... if somebody should ring —

Young Gentleman: Who'd be ringing now?

Chambermaid: But, sir ... it's so light here ...

Young Gentleman: You don't have to be bashful before me. You don't have to before anyone, anyway ... you're so pretty. I mean it, Marie, you're so ... do you know, even your hair is fragrant.

Chambermaid: Mr. Alfred ...

Young Gentleman: Don't make such a fuss, Marie ... I've seen

Marie .... ich hab' Sie schon anders auch geseh'n. Wie ich neulich in der Nacht nach Haus gekommen bin, und mir Wasser geholt hab'; da ist die Tür zu Ihrem Zimmer offen gewesen .... na ....

Das Stubenmädchen: [verbirgt ihr Gesicht.] Oh Gott, aber das hab ich gar nicht gewußt, daß der Herr Alfred so schlimm sein kann.

Der junge Herr: Da hab' ich sehr viel gesehen .... das ... und das .... und das .... und –

Das Stubenmädchen: Aber, Herr Alfred!

Der junge Herr: Komm, komm .... daher .... so, ja so ...

Das Stubenmädchen: Aber wenn jetzt wer läutet –

Der junge Herr: Jetzt hören Sie schon einmal auf .... macht man höchstens nicht auf ....

* * * * *

[Es klingelt.]

Der junge Herr: Donnerwetter .... Und was der Kerl für einen Lärm macht. – Am End' hat der schon früher geläutet und wir haben's nicht gemerkt.

Das Stubenmädchen: Oh, ich hab' alleweil aufgepaßt.

Der junge Herr: Na, so schaun S' endlich nach – durchs Guckerl. –

Das Stubenmädchen: Herr Alfred .... Sie sind aber .... nein .... so schlimm.

Der junge Herr: Bitt' Sie, schaun S' jetzt nach ....

[Das Stubenmädchen geht ab. Der junge Herr öffnet rasch die Rouleaux.]

Das Stubenmädchen [erscheint wieder.] Der ist jedenfalls schon wieder weggangen. Jetzt ist niemand mehr da. Vielleicht ist es der Doktor Schüller gewesen.

Der junge Herr: [ist unangenehm berührt.] Es ist gut. [Das Stubenmädchen nähert sich ihm. Der junge Herr entzieht sich ihr.] – Sie, Marie, – ich geh' jetzt ins Kaffeehaus.

Das Stubenmädchen: [zärtlich.] Schon .... Herr Alfred.

Der junge Herr: [streng.] Ich geh' jetzt ins Kaffeehaus. Wenn der Doktor Schüller kommen sollte –

Das Stubenmädchen: Der kommt heut' nimmer.

you worse than this. When I came home the other night and went out to get some water, the door to your room was open ... well ...

Chambermaid: [Hiding her face.] Oh my God, Mr. Alfred, I didn't think you could be so wicked.

Young Gentleman: I saw a lot, alright ... that ... and that ... and that ... and —
Chambermaid: But, Mr. Alfred!
Young Gentleman: Come, come here ... there, that's right ...
Chambermaid: But if someone should ring now —
Young Gentleman: Oh stop fussing, will you ... just let them ring ...

* * * * *

[Bell rings.]
Young Gentleman: Hell ... the fellow's making enough noise, alright ... He probably rang before and we never noticed it.
Chambermaid: Oh, I was listening all the time.
Young Gentleman: Well, you might go look anyhow ... through the peep-hole.
Chambermaid: Mr. Alfred ... honest ... you're so ... so wicked ...
Young Gentleman: Go and see who's there, will you?
[Chambermaid goes. Young gentleman raises the blinds quickly.]
Chambermaid: [Appearing again.] He must have gone away again. No one's there now. Maybe it was Doctor Schueller.
Young Gentleman: [Annoyed.] Alright. [Chambermaid comes close to him, but he draws away.] I'm going to the Café now, Marie —

Chambermaid: [Affectionately.] So soon ... Mr. Alfred.
Young Gentleman: [Sternly.] I'm going to the Café. If Doctor Schueller should come —
Chambermaid: He won't come no more today.

Der junge Herr: [noch strenger.] Wenn der Doktor Schüller
   kommen sollte, ich, ich .... ich bin — im Kaffeehaus. —
   [Geht ins andere Zimmer. Das Stubenmädchen nimmt eine
   Zigarre vom Rauchtisch, steckt sie ein und geht ab.]

Young Gentleman: [Sterner.] If Doctor Schueller should come
— I — I — I'll be at the Café.

[He goes into the next room. The Chambermaid picks up
a cigar from the table, sticks it in her mouth and goes
out.]

4: Der junge Herr und die junge Frau

Abend. — Ein mit banaler Eleganz möblierter Salon in einem Hause der Schwindgasse.

Der junge Herr ist eben eingetreten, zündet, während er noch den Hut auf dem Kopf und den Überzieher an hat, die Kerzen an. Dann öffnet er die Tür zum Nebenzimmer und wirft einen Blick hinein. Von den Kerzen des Salons geht der Lichtschein über das Parkett bis zu einem Himmelbett, das an der abschließenden Wand steht. Von dem Kamin in einer Ecke des Schlafzimmers verbreitet sich ein rötlicher Lichtschein auf die Vorhänge des Bettes. — Der junge Herr besichtigt auch das Schlafzimmer. Von dem Trumeau nimmt er einen Sprayapparat und bespritzt die Bettpolster mit feinen Strahlen von Veilchenparfüm. Dann geht er mit dem Sprayapparat durch beide Zimmer und drückt unaufhörlich auf den kleinen Ballon, so daß es bald überall nach Veilchen riecht. Dann legt er Überzieher und Hut ab. Er setzt sich auf das blausammtene Fauteuil, zündet sich eine Zigarette an und raucht. Nach einer kleinen Weile erhebt er sich wieder und vergewissert sich, daß die grünen Jalousien geschlossen sind. Plötzlich geht er wieder ins Schlafzimmer, öffnet die Lade des Nachtkästchens. Er fühlt hinein und findet eine Schildkrothaarnadel. Er sucht nach einem Ort, sie zu verstecken, gibt sie endlich in die Tasche seines Überziehers. Dann öffnet er einen Schrank, der im Salon steht, nimmt eine silberne Tasse mit einer Flasche Cognac und zwei Likörgläschen heraus, stellt alles auf den Tisch. Er geht wieder zu seinem Überzieher, aus dem er jetzt ein kleines weißes Päckchen nimmt. Er öffnet es und legt es zum Cognac;

4: The Young Gentleman and the Married Lady

Evening. A drawing room furnished with commonplace elegance in the Schwindgasse.

The young gentleman enters in hat and overcoat, and lights the candles. Then he opens the door to the adjoining room and glances into it. The candles shed a beam across the floor to a canopied bed, which stands against the wall. In one corner of the bedroom a fireplace casts a red glow on the hangings around the bed. The Young gentleman surveys the bedroom. From a tall mirror he takes an atomizer and sprays the pillows with violet perfume. He thereupon walks through both rooms spraying continually until all about him is impregnated with the odor of violets. Then he takes off his hat and overcoat, sits down on the blue velvet armchair, lights a cigarette and smokes. After a little while he rises again and makes sure that the green shutters are closed. Suddenly he goes into the bedroom, opens the drawer of the night-table, feels inside and finds a tortoise-shell hair-pin. He looks for a place to hide it in, finally sticks it in the pocket of his overcoat. Then he opens a cupboard in the drawing-room, takes out a silver tray, a bottle of Cognac and two liqueur glasses, and places them on the table. From his overcoat, then, he takes out a small white package. This he opens and lays beside the Cognac; goes back to

geht wieder zum Schrank, nimmt zwei kleine Teller und Eßbestecke heraus. Er entnimmt dem kleinen Paket eine glasierte Kastanie und ißt sie. Dann schenkt er sich ein Glas Cognac ein und trinkt es rasch aus. Dann sieht er auf seine Uhr. Er geht im Zimmer auf und ab. — Vor dem großen Wandspiegel bleibt er eine Weile stehen, richtet mit seinem Taschenkamm das Haar und den kleinen Schnurrbart. — Er geht nun zur Vorzimmertür und horcht. Nichts regt sich. Dann zieht er die blauen Portieren, die vor der Schlafzimmertür angebracht sind, zusammen. Es klingelt. Der junge Herr fährt leicht zusammen. Dann setzt er sich auf den Fauteuil und erhebt sich erst, als die Tür geöffnet wird und die junge Frau eintritt. —

Die junge Frau dicht verschleiert, schließt die Thür hinter sich, bleibt einen Augenblick stehen, indem sie die linke Hand aufs Herz legt, als müsse sie eine gewaltige Erregung bemeistern.

Der junge Herr: [tritt auf sie zu, nimmt ihre linke Hand und drückt auf den weißen, schwarz tamburierten Handschuh einen Kuß. Er sagt leise.] Ich danke Ihnen.

Die junge Frau: Alfred — Alfred!

Der junge Herr: Kommen Sie, gnädige Frau .... Kommen Sie, Frau Emma ....

Die junge Frau: Lassen Sie mich noch eine Weile — bitte .... oh bitte sehr, Alfred! [Sie steht noch immer an der Tür. Der junge Herr steht vor ihr, hält ihre Hand.] Wo bin ich denn eigentlich?

Der junge Herr: Bei mir.

Die junge Frau: Dieses Haus ist schrecklich, Alfred.

Der junge Herr: Warum denn? Es ist ein sehr vornehmes Haus.

Die junge Frau: Ich bin zwei Herren auf der Stiege begegnet.

Der junge Herr: Bekannte?

Die junge Frau: Ich weiß nicht. Es ist möglich.

Der junge Herr: Pardon, gnädige Frau — aber Sie kennen doch Ihre Bekannten.

the cupboard, and takes out two small plates, knives
and forks. He takes a marron glacé out of the package
and eats it, washing it down rapidly with a glass of
Cognac. Then he looks at his watch. He paces to and fro;
standing a while in front of the big mirror to arrange his
hair and small moustache with a pocket-comb. He goes
to the hall door and listens. No sound. Then he draws
together the blue curtains over the bedroom door. The
bell rings. The Young gentleman pulls himself quickly
together, sits down in the armchair and rises only when
the door opens and the married lady enters.

The married lady, heavily veiled, closes the door
behind her, and stands there a moment with her left
hand pressed to her heart, as if she were under violent
emotional stress.

Young Gentleman: [Goes to her, taking her gloved hand and
kissing it. In a low voice.] Thank you.

Married Lady: Alfred — Alfred!
Young Gentleman: Come, my dear ... come, Emma ...

Married Lady: Let me alone a moment — please ... Please,
Alfred! [She is still standing at the door. He faces her,
holding her hand.] Where am I? What place is this?

Young Gentleman: My rooms.
Married Lady: This is a horrible house, Alfred.
Young Gentleman: Why? It's a highly respectable house.

Married Lady: I met two men on the stairs.
Young Gentleman: Friends?
Married Lady: I don't know. Maybe.
Young Gentleman: Excuse me, my dear — but surely you
know who your friends are.

Die junge Frau: Ich habe ja gar nichts gesehen.

Der junge Herr: Aber wenn es selbst Ihre besten Freunde
waren, — sie können ja Sie nicht erkannt haben. Ich
selbst ... wenn ich nicht wüßte, daß Sie es sind .... dieser
Schleier —.

Die junge Frau: Es sind zwei.

Der junge Herr: Wollen Sie nicht ein bischen näher?.... Und
Ihren Hut legen Sie doch wenigstens ab!

Die junge Frau: Was fällt Ihnen ein, Alfred? Ich habe Ihnen
gesagt: Fünf Minuten .... Nein, länger nicht .... ich
schwöre Ihnen —

Der junge Herr: Also den Schleier —

Die junge Frau: Es sind zwei.

Der junge Herr: Nun ja, beide Schleier — ich werde Sie doch
wenigstens sehen dürfen.

Die junge Frau: Haben Sie mich denn lieb, Alfred?

Der junge Herr: [tief verletzt.] Emma — Sie fragen mich ....

Die junge Frau: Es ist hier so heiß.

Der junge Herr: Aber Sie haben ja Ihre Pelzmantille an — Sie
werden sich wahrhaftig verkühlen.

Die junge Frau: [tritt endlich ins Zimmer, wirft sich auf den
Fauteuil.] Ich bin totmüd'.

Der junge Herr: Erlauben Sie. [Er nimmt ihr die Schleier
ab; nimmt die Nadel aus ihrem Hut, legt Hut, Nadel,
Schleier beiseite. Die junge Frau läßt es geschehen. Der
junge Herr steht vor ihr, schüttelt den Kopf.]

Die junge Frau: Was haben Sie?

Der junge Herr: So schön waren Sie noch nie.

Die junge Frau: Wieso?

Der junge Herr: Allein .... allein mit Ihnen — Emma — [Er
läßt sich neben ihrem Fauteuil nieder, auf ein Knie,
nimmt ihre beiden Hände und bedeckt sie mit Küssen.]

Die junge Frau: Und jetzt .... lassen Sie mich wieder gehen.
Was Sie von mir verlangt haben, hab' ich getan. [Der
junge Herr läßt seinen Kopf auf ihren Schoß sinken.]
Sie haben mir versprochen, brav zu sein.

Der junge Herr: Ja.

Married Lady: But I couldn't see a thing.

Young Gentleman: Well, even if they were your best friends they couldn't have recognized you. Even I ... if I didn't know it was you ... that veil —

Married Lady: There are two of them.

Young Gentleman: Aren't you going to come a little nearer? ... At least you could take you hat off!

Married Lady: Are you mad, Alfred? I told you: five minutes ... No, not a minute more ... I swear —

Young Gentleman: Well, then, the veil —

Married Lady: There are two.

Young Gentleman: Alright, both veils — you could let me see you, at least.

Married Lady: Do you really love me, Alfred?

Young Gentleman: [Deeply hurt.] Emma — how can you ask ...

Married Lady: It's so hot here.

Young Gentleman: You've got your fur coat on — you'll surely catch cold.

Married Lady: [Finally walking into the room, sinking into the armchair.] I'm dead tired.

Young Gentleman: Allow me. [Takes off her veils, takes the pin out of her hat, puts hat, pin and veils aside. Married lady does not demur. He stands in front of her, shaking his head.]

Married Lady: What's the matter?

Young Gentleman: You've never looked so beautiful.

Married Lady: Really?

Young Gentleman: Alone ... alone with you — Emma — [He sinks on his knees by the armchair, takes both her hands and covers them with kisses.]

Married Lady: Now — now you must let me go again. I've done what you wanted me to. [Young gentleman lets his head sink on her lap.] You promised me you'd be good.

Young Gentleman: Yes.

Die junge Frau: Man erstickt in diesem Zimmer.

Der junge Herr: [steht auf.] Noch haben Sie Ihre Mantille an.

Die junge Frau: Legen Sie sie zu meinem Hut. [Der junge Herr nimmt ihr die Mantille ab und legt sie gleichfalls auf den Divan.] Und jetzt — adieu —

Der junge Herr: Emma —! — Emma! —

Die junge Frau: Die fünf Minuten sind längst vorbei.

Der junge Herr: Noch nicht eine! —

Die junge Frau: Alfred, sagen Sie mir einmal ganz genau, wie spät es ist.

Der junge Herr: Es ist punkt viertel sieben.

Die junge Frau: Jetzt sollte ich längst bei meiner Schwester sein.

Der junge Herr: Ihre Schwester können Sie oft sehen ....

Die junge Frau: Oh Gott, Alfred, warum haben Sie mich dazu verleitet.

Der junge Herr: Weil ich Sie .... anbete, Emma.

Die junge Frau: Wie vielen haben Sie das schon gesagt?

Der junge Herr: Seit ich Sie gesehen, niemandem.

Die junge Frau: Was bin ich für eine leichtsinnige Person! Wer mir das vorausgesagt hätte ... noch vor acht Tagen ... noch gestern ...

Der junge Herr: Und vorgestern haben Sie mir ja schon versprochen ...

Die junge Frau: Sie haben mich so gequält. Aber ich habe es nicht tun wollen. Gott ist mein Zeuge — ich habe es nicht tun wollen ... Gestern war ich fest entschlossen ... Wissen Sie, daß ich Ihnen gestern Abends sogar einen langen Brief geschrieben habe?

Der junge Herr: Ich habe keinen bekommen.

Die junge Frau: Ich habe ihn wieder zerrissen. Oh, ich hätte Ihnen lieber diesen Brief schicken sollen.

Der junge Herr: Es ist doch besser so.

Die junge Frau: Oh nein, es ist schändlich ... von mir. Ich begreife mich selber nicht. Adieu, Alfred, lassen Sie mich. [Der junge Herr umfaßt sie und bedeckt ihr Gesicht mit heißen Küssen.] So ... halten Sie Ihr Wort ...

Married Lady: It's suffocating in this room.

Young Gentleman: [Standing up.] You still have your coat on.

Married Lady: Put it next to my hat. [Young gentleman takes her coat off and lays it on the sofa.] And now — adieu —

Young Gentleman: Emma! Emma!

Married Lady: The five minutes were up long ago.

Young Gentleman: Not even one!

Married Lady: Alfred, tell me exactly what time it is.

Young Gentleman: It's exactly quarter past six.

Married Lady: I should have been at my sister's long ago.

Young Gentleman: Your sister can see you often ...

Married Lady: Oh God, Alfred, why have you made me do this?

Young Gentleman: Because I — adore you, Emma.

Married Lady: How many others have you said that to?

Young Gentleman: Since I've known you — no one.

Married Lady: What a frivolous creature I am! If anyone had told me ... a week ago ... or even yesterday ...

Young Gentleman: And day before yesterday you'd already promised me ...

Married Lady: You tormented me so. But I didn't want to do it. God is my witness — I didn't want to do it ... Yesterday I was absolutely determined ... Do you know, I even wrote you a long letter last night!

Young Gentleman: I didn't receive any.

Married Lady: I tore it up. Oh, I should have sent you that letter!

Young Gentleman: I'm glad you didn't.

Married Lady: Oh no, it's disgraceful ... of me. I can't make myself out. Goodbye, Alfred, let me go. [Young gentleman takes her in his arms and covers her face with passionate kisses.] Is this how you keep your promise? ...

Der junge Herr: Noch einen Kuß — noch einen.

Die junge Frau: Den letzten. [Er küßt sie; sie erwidert den Kuß; ihre Lippen bleiben lange aneinandergeschlossen.]

Der junge Herr: Soll ich Ihnen etwas sagen, Emma? Ich weiß jetzt erst, was Glück ist. [Die junge Frau sinkt in ein Fauteuil zurück. Der junge Herr setzt sich auf die Lehne, schlingt einen Arm leicht um ihren Nacken.] .... oder vielmehr ich weiß jetzt erst, was Glück sein könnte. [Die junge Frau seufzt tief auf. Der junge Herr küßt sie wieder.]

Die junge Frau: Alfred, Alfred, was machen Sie aus mir!

Der junge Herr: Nicht wahr — es ist hier gar nicht so ungemütlich ... Und wir sind ja hier so sicher! Es ist doch tausendmal schöner als diese Rendezvous im Freien ...

Die junge Frau: Oh, erinnern Sie mich nur nicht daran.

Der junge Herr: Ich werde auch daran immer mit tausend Freuden denken. Für mich ist jede Minute, die ich an Ihrer Seite verbringen durfte, eine süße Erinnerung.

Die junge Frau: Erinnern Sie sich noch an den Industriellenball?

Der junge Herr: Ob ich mich daran erinnere ...? Da bin ich ja während des Soupers neben Ihnen gesessen, ganz nahe neben Ihnen. Ihr Mann hat Champagner ... [Die junge Frau sieht ihn klagend an.] Ich wollte nur vom Champagner reden. Sagen Sie, Emma, wollen Sie nicht ein Glas Cognac trinken?

Die junge Frau: Einen Tropfen, aber geben Sie mir vorher ein Glas Wasser.

Der junge Herr: Ja ... Wo ist denn nur — ach ja ... [Er schlägt die Portière zurück und geht ins Schlafzimmer. Die junge Frau sieht ihm nach. Der junge Herr kommt zurück mit einer Karaffe Wasser und zwei Trinkgläsern.]

Die junge Frau: Wo waren Sie denn?

Der junge Herr: Im ... Nebenzimmer. [Schenkt ein Glas Wasser ein.]

Die junge Frau: Jetzt werde ich Sie etwas fragen, Alfred — und schwören Sie mir, daß Sie mir die Wahrheit sagen werden.

Young Gentleman: One more kiss — just one.

Married Lady: The last one. [He kisses her, she responds; their lips are joined for a long time.]

Young Gentleman: Shall I tell you something, Emma? Now I know what happiness is, for the first time. [Married lady sinks back into the armchair. He sits on the arm, his arm lightly encircling her back.] ... or rather, I know now what happiness might be. [Married lady sighs deeply. He kisses her again.]

Married Lady: Alfred, Alfred, what are you doing to me?

Young Gentleman: It's not all bad here, is it, Emma? ... And we're so safe here. After all, it's a thousand times nicer than those meetings outside.

Married Lady: Oh, don't remind me of them.

Young Gentleman: But I shall always think of them with great delight. Every minute I'm allowed by your side is a sweet memory to me.

Married Lady: Do you remember the Charity Ball?

Young Gentleman: Do I remember it! Why, I was sitting near you all during supper, right near you. Your husband had champagne ... [Married lady looks at him reproachfully.] I was only going to speak about the champagne. By the way, Emma, wouldn't you like a glass of Cognac?

Married Lady: Just a drop, but first give me a glass of water.

Young Gentleman: Certainly ... where is that ... Oh yes, ... [He draws aside the curtains and goes into the bedroom, She looks after him. Young gentleman comes back with a carafe of water and two glasses.]

Married Lady: Where were you?

Young Gentleman: In the ... next room. [Pours a glass of water.]

Married Lady: I'm going to ask you something, Alfred — and you've got to swear you'll answer the truth.

Der junge Herr: Ich schwöre. —

Die junge Frau: War in diesen Räumen schon jemals eine andere Frau?

Der junge Herr: Aber Emma — dieses Haus steht schon zwanzig Jahre! —

Die junge Frau: Sie wissen, was ich meine, Alfred ... Mit Ihnen! Bei Ihnen!

Der junge Herr: Mit mir — hier — Emma! — Es ist nicht schön, daß Sie an so etwas denken können.

Die junge Frau: Also Sie haben .... wie soll ich .... Aber nein, ich will Sie lieber nicht fragen. Es ist besser, wenn ich nicht frage. Ich bin ja selbst schuld. Alles rächt sich.

Der junge Herr: Ja, was haben Sie denn? Was ist Ihnen denn? Was rächt sich?

Die junge Frau: Nein, nein, nein, ich darf nicht zum Bewußtsein kommen ... Sonst müßte ich vor Scham in die Erde sinken.

Der junge Herr: [mit der Karaffe Wasser in der Hand, schüttelt traurig den Kopf.] Emma, wenn Sie ahnen könnten, wie weh' Sie mir tun. [Die junge Frau schenkt sich ein Glas Cognac ein.] Ich will Ihnen etwas sagen, Emma. Wenn Sie sich schämen, hier zu sein — wenn ich Ihnen also gleichgültig bin — wenn Sie nicht fühlen, daß Sie für mich alle Seligkeit der Welt bedeuten — so geh'n Sie lieber. —

Die junge Frau: Ja, das werd' ich auch tun.

Der junge Herr: [sie bei der Hand fassend.] Wenn Sie aber ahnen, daß ich ohne Sie nicht leben kann, daß ein Kuß auf Ihre Hand für mich mehr bedeutet, als alle Zärtlichkeiten, die alle Frauen auf der ganzen Welt .... Emma, ich bin nicht wie die anderen jungen Leute, die den Hof machen können — ich bin vielleicht zu naiv .... ich ....

Die junge Frau: Wenn Sie aber doch sind wie die anderen jungen Leute?

Der junge Herr: Dann wären Sie heute nicht da — denn Sie sind nicht wie die anderen Frauen.

Die junge Frau: Woher wissen Sie das?

Young Gentleman: I swear —

Married Lady: Has any other woman ever been in these rooms?

Young Gentleman: But, Emma — this house was built twenty years ago!

Married Lady: You know perfectly well what I mean, Alfred ... With you! In your rooms!

Young Gentleman: Here — with me — Emma? Really, it isn't very nice of you to think of such things.

Married Lady: Oh, so you have ... how shall I say ... No, I'd rather not ask you. It's better not to. It's my fault, anyway. One pays for everything.

Young Gentleman: What do you mean? What's the matter? Who pays for what?

Married Lady: No, no, no, I mustn't return to consciousness ... otherwise I'd die of shame.

Young Gentleman: [Shaking his head sadly, the water carafe in his hand.] Emma, if you only knew how you are hurting me. [Married lady pours herself a glass of Cognac.] I want to tell you something, Emma. If you are ashamed to be here — if I mean nothing to you — if you don't feel that you mean all the bliss in the world to me — then you'd better go.

Married Lady: Yes — I mean to.

Young Gentleman: [Taking her hand.] But if you'd only realize that I can't live without you, that the mere kissing of your hand means more to me than all the caresses of all the women in the world ... Emma, I'm not like the other young men who can play at love — perhaps I'm too naive ...

Married Lady: But suppose you really are like other men?

Young Gentleman: Then you wouldn't be here now — because you're not like other women.

Married Lady: How did you know that?

Der junge Herr: [hat sie zum Divan gezogen, sich nahe neben
    sie gesetzt.] Ich habe viel über Sie nachgedacht. Ich
    weiß, Sie sind unglücklich.
Die junge Frau: [erfreut.] Ja.
Der junge Herr: Das Leben ist so leer, so nichtig — und dann,
    — so kurz — so entsetzlich kurz! Es gibt nur ein Glück
    .... einen Menschen finden, von dem man geliebt wird
    — [Die junge Frau hat eine kandierte Birne vom Tisch
    genommen, nimmt sie in den Mund.] Mir die Hälfte!
    [Sie reicht sie ihm mit den Lippen.]
Die junge Frau: [faßt die Hände des jungen Herrn, die sich zu
    verirren drohen.] Was tun Sie denn, Alfred .... Ist das
    Ihr Versprechen.
Der junge Herr: [die Birne verschluckend, dann kühner.] Das
    Leben ist so kurz.
Die junge Frau: [schwach.] Aber das ist ja kein Grund —
Der junge Herr: [mechanisch.] Oh ja.
Die junge Frau: [schwächer.] Schauen Sie Alfred, und Sie
    haben doch versprochen, brav .... Und es ist so hell ....
Der junge Herr: Komm', komm', du einzige, einzige .... [Er
    hebt sie vom Divan empor.]
Die junge Frau: Was machen Sie denn?
Der junge Herr: Da d'rin ist es gar nicht hell.
Die junge Frau: Ist denn da noch ein Zimmer?
Der junge Herr: [zieht sie mit.] Ein schönes .... und ganz
    dunkel.
Die junge Frau: Bleiben wir doch lieber hier. [Der junge Herr
    bereits mit ihr hinter der Portière, im Schlafzimmer,
    nestelt ihr die Taille auf.] Sie sind so .... oh Gott, was
    machen Sie aus mir! — Alfred!
Der junge Herr: Ich bete dich an, Emma!
Die junge Frau: So wart' doch, wart' doch wenigstens ....
    [Schwach.] Geh' .... ich ruf dich dann.
Der junge Herr: Laß mir dich — laß dir mich [er verspricht
    sich.] .... laß .... mich — dir — helfen.
Die junge Frau: Du zerreißt mir ja alles.
Der junge Herr: Du hast kein Mieder an?
Die junge Frau: Ich trag' nie ein Mieder. Die Odilon trägt auch

Young Gentleman: [Drawing her onto the sofa, sitting next to her.] I've thought a great deal about you. I know that you're unhappy.

Married Lady: [Pleased.] Yes.

Young Gentleman: Life is so empty, so meaningless — and then — so short — so appallingly short! There's only one happiness ... to find someone who loves you — [Married lady takes a candied pear from the table and puts it in her mouth.] Give me half! [She gives it to him with her lips.]

Married Lady: [Takes the Young gentleman's hands which have begun to stray.] What are you doing, Alfred? ... What about your promise?

Young Gentleman: [Swallowing the pear, then bolder.] Life is so short.

Married Lady: [Weakly.] But surely that's no reason —

Young Gentleman: [Mechanically.] Oh yes.

Married Lady: [Weaker still.] Really, Alfred, you did promise ... be good ... And it's so light ...

Young Gentleman: Oh come, come ... my only one, my darling ... [He lifts her up from the sofa.]

Married Lady: What are you doing?

Young Gentleman: It's not at all light in there.

Married Lady: Is there another room?

Young Gentleman: [Drawing her after him.] A charming one ... and quite dark.

Married Lady: I think we'd better stay here. [Young gentleman, already leading her beyond the curtains and into the bedroom, unfastens her bodice.] You're so ... Heavens, what are you doing to me, Alfred!

Young Gentleman: I adore you, Emma!

Married Lady: But wait — wait a minute ... [Weakly.] Go ... I'll call you.

Young Gentleman: Let me — let you — [Fussed.] — I mean, can't I — help you —

Married Lady: You're tearing everything.

Young Gentleman: You don't wear corsets?

Married Lady: I never wear corsets. Neither does Ida

keines. Aber die Schuh' kannst du mir aufknöpfeln.
[Der junge Herr knöpfelt die Schuhe auf, küßt ihre
Füße. Die junge Frau: ist ins Bett geschlüpft.] Oh mir
ist kalt.

Der junge Herr: Gleich wird's warm werden.

Die junge Frau: [leise lachend.] Glaubst du?

Der junge Herr: [unangenehm berührt, für sich.] Das hätte
sie nicht sagen sollen. [Entkleidet sich im Dunkel.]

Die junge Frau: [zärtlich.] Komm, komm, komm!

Der junge Herr: [dadurch wieder in besserer Stimmung.]
Gleich —

Die junge Frau: Es riecht hier so nach Veilchen.

Der junge Herr: Das bist du selbst .... Ja [zu ihr.] du selbst.

Die junge Frau: Alfred .... Alfred!!!!

Der junge Herr: Emma ....

* * * * *

Der junge Herr: Ich habe dich offenbar zu lieb .... ja .... ich bin
wie von Sinnen.

Die junge Frau ......

Der junge Herr: Die ganzen Tage über bin ich schon wie
verrückt. Ich hab es geahnt.

Die junge Frau: Mach' dir nichts draus.

Der junge Herr: Oh gewiß nicht. Es ist ja geradezu
selbstverständlich, wenn man ....

Die junge Frau: Nicht .... nicht .... Du bist nervös. Beruhige
dich nur ....

Der junge Herr: Kennst du Stendhal?

Die junge Frau: Stendhal?

Der junge Herr: Die psychologie de l'amour.

Die junge Frau: Nein, warum fragst du mich?

Der junge Herr: Da kommt eine Geschichte drin vor, die sehr
bezeichnend ist.

Die junge Frau: Was ist das für eine Geschichte?

Der junge Herr: Das ist eine ganze Gesellschaft von
Kavallerieoffizieren zusammen —

Die junge Frau: So.

Der junge Herr: Und die erzählen von ihren Liebesabenteuern.
Und jeder berichtet, daß ihm bei der Frau, die er am

Rubinstein. But you might unbutton my shoes. [Young gentleman unbuttons her shoes, kisses her feet. She slips into bed.] Oh, I'm cold.

Young Gentleman: You'll soon be warm.

Married Lady: [Laughing softly.] Think so!

Young Gentleman: [Vaguely annoyed, to himself.] She needn't have said that. [Undresses in the dark.]

Married Lady: [Tenderly.] Come, come, come.

Young Gentleman: [Now in a better mood.] Right away —

Married Lady: It smells so of violets here.

Young Gentleman: That's you yourself ... Yes [To her.] you yourself.

Married Lady: Alfred ... Alfred!!!

Young Gentleman: Emma ...

* * * * *

Young Gentleman: It's obvious that I love you too much ... yes ... beyond all reason.

Married Lady: ... ...

Young Gentleman: For days I've been going about like mad. I had a feeling this would happen.

Married Lady: Don't worry about it.

Young Gentleman: Oh, of course not. After all, it's only natural when ...

Married Lady: Don't ... don't ... You're just nervous. Calm yourself ...

Young Gentleman: Do you know Stendhal?

Married Lady: Stendhal?

Young Gentleman: The Psychology of Love.

Married Lady: No, why do you ask me?

Young Gentleman: There's a story in it that's very significant.

Married Lady: What kind of story?

Young Gentleman: Well, there's a gathering of cavalry officers —

Married Lady: Yes ...

Young Gentleman: And they're telling about their love affairs. And every one of them says that when they were with

meisten, weißt du, am leidenschaftlichsten geliebt hat
.... daß ihn die, daß er die — also kurz und gut, daß es
jedem bei dieser Frau so gegangen ist, wie jetzt mir.

Die junge Frau: Ja.

Der junge Herr: Das ist sehr charakteristisch.

Die junge Frau: Ja.

Der junge Herr: Es ist noch nicht aus. Ein einziger behauptet
.... es sei ihm in seinem ganzen Leben noch nicht
passiert, aber, setzt Stendhal hinzu — das war ein
berüchtigter Bramarbas.

Die junge Frau: So. —

Der junge Herr: Und doch verstimmt es einen, das ist das
Dumme, so gleichgiltig es eigentlich ist.

Die junge Frau: Freilich. Überhaupt weißt du .... du hast mir
ja versprochen, brav zu sein.

Der junge Herr: Geh', nicht lachen, das bessert die Sache
nicht.

Die junge Frau: Aber nein, ich lache ja nicht. Das von Stendhal
ist wirklich interessant. Ich habe immer gedacht, daß
nur bei älteren .... oder bei sehr .... weißt du, bei Leuten,
die viel gelebt haben ....

Der junge Herr: Was fällt dir ein. Das hat damit gar nichts
zu tun. Ich habe übrigens die hübscheste Geschichte
aus dem Stendhal ganz vergessen. Da ist einer von
den Kavallerieoffizieren, der erzählt sogar, daß er drei
Nächte oder gar sechs .... ich weiß nicht mehr, mit der
Frau zusammen war, die er durch Wochen hindurch
verlangt hat — desirée — verstehst du — und die
haben alle diese Nächte hindurch nichts getan als vor
Glück geweint .... beide ....

Die junge Frau: Beide?

Der junge Herr: Ja. Wundert dich das? Ich find' das so
begreiflich — gerade wenn man sich liebt.

Die junge Frau: Aber es gibt gewiß viele, die nicht weinen.

Der junge Herr: [nervös.] Gewiß .... das ist ja auch ein
exceptioneller Fall.

Die junge Frau: Ah — ich dachte, Stendhal sagte, alle
Kavallerieoffiziere weinen bei dieser Gelegenheit.

the woman they loved most deeply, you know, most passionately ... well, that she — that he — well, to make a long story short, that in spite of loving this woman so, the same thing happened as with me, just now.

Married Lady: Yes.

Young Gentleman: That's very characteristic.

Married Lady: Yes.

Young Gentleman: That's not the end of it yet. One of them claims that it's never happened to him in his whole life, but Stendhal remarks that he was a notorious liar.

Married Lady: I see.

Young Gentleman: Even so, it depresses one, in spite of its unimportance — That's the stupid part of it.

Married Lady: Of course. Anyway, you know, you did promise to be good.

Young Gentleman: Now don't laugh, that doesn't help.

Married Lady: But I'm not laughing. That Stendhal thing is very interesting. Although I always thought that only older men ... or very ... you know, people who've indulged in excesses ...

Young Gentleman: What an idea! That has absolutely nothing to do with it. But I forgot to tell you the best of Stendhal's stories. One of those cavalry officers actually said that he'd spent three nights, or even six, with the woman he had passionately desired ... longed for, you know — for weeks — and all they did on every one of those nights together was to weep for joy ... both of them ...

Married Lady: Both?

Young Gentleman: Yes. Does that surprise you? It seems perfectly comprehensible to me — especially when one's in love.

Married Lady: But surely, there must be many who don't weep.

Young Gentleman: [Nervously.] Certainly ... and that was an exceptional case, of course.

Married Lady: Oh, I thought Stendhal said that all cavalry officers weep on such occasions.

Der junge Herr: Siehst du, jetzt machst du dich doch lustig.

Die junge Frau: Aber was fällt dir ein! Sei doch nicht kindisch, Alfred!

Der junge Herr: Es macht nun einmal nervös .... Dabei habe ich die Empfindung, daß du ununterbrochen daran denkst. Das geniert mich erst recht.

Die junge Frau: Ich denke absolut nicht daran.

Der junge Herr: Oh ja. Wenn ich nur überzeugt wäre, daß du mich liebst.

Die junge Frau: Verlangst du noch mehr Beweise?

Der junge Herr: Siehst du ... immer machst du dich lustig.

Die junge Frau: Wieso denn? Komm', gib mir dein süßes Kopferl.

Der junge Herr: Ach, das tut wohl.

Die junge Frau: Hast du mich lieb?

Der junge Herr: Oh, ich bin ja so glücklich.

Die junge Frau: Aber du brauchst nicht auch noch zu weinen.

Der junge Herr: [sich von ihr entfernend, höchst irritiert.] Wieder, wieder. Ich hab dich ja so gebeten ....

Die junge Frau: Wenn ich dir sage, daß du nicht weinen sollst ...

Der junge Herr: Du hast gesagt: Auch noch zu weinen.

Die junge Frau: Du bist nervös, mein Schatz.

Der junge Herr: Das weiß ich.

Die junge Frau: Aber du sollst es nicht sein. Es ist mir sogar lieb, daß es .... daß wir sozusagen als gute Kameraden...

Der junge Herr: Schon wieder fangst du an.

Die junge Frau: Erinnerst du dich denn nicht! Das war eines unserer ersten Gespräche. Gute Kameraden haben wir sein wollen; nichts weiter. Oh, das war schön ..... das war bei meiner Schwester, im Jänner auf dem großen Ball, während der Quadrille .... Um Gotteswillen, ich sollte ja längst fort sein .... meine Schwester erwartet mich ja — was werd' ich ihr denn sagen .... Adieu, Alfred —

Der junge Herr: Emma —! so willst du mich verlassen!

Die junge Frau: Ja — so! —

Der junge Herr: Noch fünf Minuten ....

Young Gentleman: Now you're making fun again.
Married Lady: Not at all! Don't be childish, Alfred!

Young Gentleman: Well, it does get on one's nerves ... Besides,
 I have a feeling that you keep thinking about it all the
 time. That upsets me a lot.
Married Lady: I'm not thinking of it at all.
Young Gentleman: If only I could be convinced of your love.

Married Lady: Do you still demand proofs?
Young Gentleman: There you are — always joking.
Married Lady: How so? Come, put your handsome head
 here.
Young Gentleman: Ah, that feels good.
Married Lady: Do you love me?
Young Gentleman: Oh, I am so happy.
Married Lady: But you don't need to cry too, do you?
Young Gentleman: [Drawing away from her, highly irritated.]
 There you are again, the same old thing. I begged you
 so ...
Married Lady: But I only said that you needn't cry ...
Young Gentleman: You said: 'needn't cry too.'
Married Lady: Darling, you're wrought up.
Young Gentleman: I know I am.
Married Lady: But you shouldn't be. In fact, I like us to be —
 well — sort of good friends ...
Young Gentleman: There you go again.
Married Lady: But don't you remember? That was one of our
 first conversations together. We were going to be good
 friends; nothing more. Oh, that was beautiful ... we
 were at my sister's, at that big ball in January, dancing
 the quadrille... . Good heavens, I should have gone
 long ago ... my sister's expecting me ... what shall I say
 to her ... Adieu, Alfred —

Young Gentleman: Emma! You're going to leave me like this?
Married Lady: Yes!
Young Gentleman: Five minutes more ...

Die junge Frau: Gut. Noch fünf Minuten. Aber du mußt mir versprechen .... dich nicht zu rühren? ... Ja?... Ich will dir noch einen Kuß zum Abschied geben ..... Pst .... ruhig .... nicht rühren, hab ich gesagt, sonst steh ich gleich auf, du mein süßer ... süßer ...

Der junge Herr: Emma .... meine ange........

* * * * *

Die junge Frau: Mein Alfred —

Der junge Herr: Ah, bei dir ist der Himmel.

Die junge Frau: Aber jetzt muß ich wirklich fort.

Der junge Herr: Ach, laß deine Schwester warten.

Die junge Frau: Nach Haus muß ich. Für meine Schwester ist's längst zu spät. Wie viel Uhr ist es denn eigentlich?

Der junge Herr: Ja, wie soll ich das eruieren?

Die junge Frau: Du musst eben auf die Uhr sehen.

Der junge Herr: Meine Uhr ist in meinem Gilet.

Die junge Frau: So hol' sie.

Der junge Herr: [steht mit einem mächtigen Ruck auf.] Acht.

Die junge Frau: [erhebt sich rasch.] Um Gotteswillen .... Rasch, Alfred, gib mir meine Strümpfe. Was soll ich denn nur sagen? Zu Hause wird man sicher schon auf mich warten ... acht Uhr ....

Der junge Herr: Wann seh' ich dich denn wieder?

Die junge Frau: Nie.

Der junge Herr: Emma! Hast du mich denn nicht mehr lieb?

Die junge Frau: Eben darum. Gib mir meine Schuhe.

Der junge Herr: Niemals wieder? Hier sind die Schuhe.

Die junge Frau: In meinem Sack ist ein Schuhknöpfler. Ich bitt' dich, rasch ....

Der junge Herr: Hier ist der Knöpfler.

Die junge Frau: Alfred, das kann uns beide den Hals kosten.

Der junge Herr: [höchst unangenehm berührt.] Wieso?

Die junge Frau: Ja, was soll ich denn sagen, wenn er mich fragt: Woher kommst du?

Der junge Herr: Von der Schwester.

Die junge Frau: Ja, wenn ich lügen könnte.

Der junge Herr: Na, du mußt es eben tun.

Die junge Frau: Alles für so einen Menschen. Ach, komm her

Married Lady: Very well. Five minutes more. But you must promise not to — to stir. Yes? ... I'll just give you a goodbye kiss. No, no ... quiet, I said ... don't budge, or else I'll get right up, you darling ... darling ...

Young Gentleman: Emma ... my adorable ...

* * * * *

Married Lady: My Alfred —

Young Gentleman: Oh, it's heaven to be with you.

Married Lady: But I really must go now.

Young Gentleman: Oh, let your sister wait.

Married Lady: I've got to go home. It's much too late for my sister's now. What time is it, anyway?

Young Gentleman: How should I know?

Married Lady: You might just look at your watch.

Young Gentleman: My watch is in my vest.

Married Lady: Well, go get it.

Young Gentleman: [Rises with a mighty effort.] Eight.

Married Lady: [Quickly rising.] Good heavens ... Quick, Alfred, hand me my stockings. What on earth shall I say? They're undoubtedly waiting for me at home ... eight o' clock.

Young Gentleman: When will I see you again?

Married Lady: Never.

Young Gentleman: Emma! Then you don't love me anymore?

Married Lady: That's just it. Give me my shoes.

Young Gentleman: Never again? Here are your shoes.

Married Lady: There's a button-hook in my bag. Get it, please, quick ...

Young Gentleman: Here's the button-hook.

Married Lady: Alfred, this may ruin us both.

Young Gentleman: [Very disagreeably affected.] How so?

Married Lady: Well, what shall I say when he asks me where I've been?

Young Gentleman: At your sister's.

Married Lady: Yes, if I could lie.

Young Gentleman: Well, you'll just have to.

Married Lady: And all this for such a man. Oh, come here ...

.... laß dich noch einmal küssen. [Sie umarmt ihn.] —
Und jetzt — laß mich allein, geh' ins andere Zimmer.
Ich kann mich nicht anziehen, wenn du dabei bist. [Der
junge Herr geht in den Salon, wo er sich ankleidet. Er
ißt etwas von der Bäckerei, trinkt ein Glas Cognac. Die
junge Frau ruft nach einer Weile.] Alfred!

Der junge Herr: Mein Schatz.

Die junge Frau: Es ist doch besser, daß wir nicht geweint
haben.

Der junge Herr: [nicht ohne Stolz lächelnd.] Wie kann man
so frivol reden? —

Die junge Frau: Wie wird das jetzt nur sein — wenn wir uns
zufällig wieder einmal in Gesellschaft begegnen?

Der junge Herr: Zufällig — einmal .... Du bist ja morgen
sicher auch bei Lobheimers?

Die junge Frau: Ja. Du auch?

Der junge Herr: Freilich. Darf ich dich um den Kotillion
bitten?

Die junge Frau: Oh, ich werde nicht hinkommen. Was glaubst
du denn? — Ich würde ja ... [sie tritt völlig angekleidet
in den Salon, nimmt eine Chokoladebäckerei.] in die
Erde sinken.

Der junge Herr: Also morgen bei Lobheimer, das ist schön.

Die junge Frau: Nein, nein .... ich sage ab; bestimmt —

Der junge Herr: Also übermorgen .... hier.

Die junge Frau: Was fällt dir ein?

Der junge Herr: Um sechs ....

Die junge Frau: Hier an der Ecke stehen Wagen, nicht wahr?

Der junge Herr: Ja, so viel du willst. Also übermorgen hier
um sechs. So sag' doch ja, mein geliebter Schatz.

Die junge Frau: .... Das besprechen wir morgen beim Kotillion.

Der junge Herr: [umarmt sie.] Mein Engel.

Die junge Frau: Nicht wieder meine Frisur ruinieren.

Der junge Herr: Also morgen bei Lobheimers und
übermorgen in meinen Armen.

Die junge Frau: Leb wohl ....

Der junge Herr: [plötzlich wieder besorgt.] Und was wirst
du — ihm heut sagen? —

I want to give you just one more kiss. [She embraces him.] And now — leave me alone and go into the other room, I can't dress when you're around. [Young gentleman goes into living-room, where he dresses, eats pastry and drinks a glass of Cognac. Presently she calls.] Alfred!

Young Gentleman: Yes, sweet?

Married Lady: After all it was much better that we didn't weep.

Young Gentleman: [Not without pride, smiling.] How can you be so frivolous?

Married Lady: What are we to do if we happen to meet accidentally at some party again?

Young Gentleman: Accidentally ... But surely you'll be at the Lobheimers too tomorrow, won't you?

Married Lady: Yes. And you too?

Young Gentleman: Certainly. May I have the first dance?

Married Lady: Oh, I shan't go. What are you thinking of? Why I'd ... [Walks into living room, fully dressed, takes a chocolate tart.] I'd sink right through the floor for shame.

Young Gentleman: Well, at the Lobheimers then, tomorrow. That's fine.

Married Lady: No, no ... I won't go ... definitely not.

Young Gentleman: Well, then, day after tomorrow ... here.

Married Lady: Are you mad?

Young Gentleman: At six ...

Married Lady: There are taxis at this corner, aren't there?

Young Gentleman: Yes, all you want. All right then, day after tomorrow, here, at six. Say yes, my adorable sweet.

Married Lady: ... We'll talk it over tomorrow at the dance.

Young Gentleman: [Embracing her.] My own beloved.

Married Lady: Don't muss my hair again.

Young Gentleman: Tomorrow at the Lobheimers then, and the day after in my arms.

Married Lady: Goodbye ...

Young Gentleman: [Suddenly worried again.] But what will you say to him — now?

Die junge Frau: Frag' nicht .... frag' nicht .... es ist zu
   schrecklich. — Warum hab' ich dich so lieb! — Adieu.
   — Wenn ich wieder Menschen auf der Stiege begegne,
   trifft mich der Schlag. — Pah! —
[Der junge Herr küßt ihr noch einmal die Hand. Die junge
   Frau geht.]
Der junge Herr: [bleibt allein zurück. Dann setzt er sich auf
   den Divan. Er lächelt vor sich hin und sagt zu sich
   selbst.] Also jetzt hab' ich ein Verhältnis mit einer
   anständigen Frau.

Married Lady: Don't ask me ... don't ask ... it's all too horrible ... Why do I love you so? — Adieu. — If I meet people on the stairs again I'll have heart failure.

[Young gentleman kisses her hand once again. married lady goes.]

Young Gentleman: [Alone, sits on the sofa, chuckles to himself and murmurs softly.] Well, at least I'm having an affair with a respectable woman.

5: Die junge Frau und der Ehemann

Ein behagliches Schlafgemach. Es ist halb elf Uhr Nachts. Die Frau liegt zu Bette und liest. Der Gatte tritt eben, im Schlafrock, ins Zimmer.

Die junge Frau: [ohne aufzuschauen.] Du arbeitest nicht mehr?

Der Gatte: Nein. Ich bin zu müde. Und außerdem ...

Die junge Frau: Nun? —

Der Gatte: Ich hab' mich an meinem Schreibtisch plötzlich so einsam gefühlt. Ich habe Sehnsucht nach dir bekommen.

Die junge Frau: [schaut auf.] Wirklich?

Der Gatte: [setzt sich zu ihr aufs Bett.] Lies heute nicht mehr. Du wirst dir die Augen verderben.

Die junge Frau: [schlägt das Buch zu.] Was hast du denn?

Der Gatte: Nichts, mein Kind. Verliebt bin ich in dich! Das weißt du ja!

Die junge Frau: Man könnte es manchmal fast vergessen.

Der Gatte: Man muß es sogar manchmal vergessen.

Die junge Frau: Warum?

Der Gatte: Weil die Ehe sonst etwas unvollkommenes wäre. Sie würde .... wie soll ich nur sagen .... sie würde ihre Heiligkeit verlieren.

Die junge Frau: Oh ....

Der Gatte: Glaube mir — es ist so .... Hätten wir in den fünf Jahren, die wir jetzt miteinander verheiratet sind, nicht manchmal vergessen, daß wir ineinander verliebt sind — wir wären es wohl gar nicht mehr.

Die junge Frau: Das ist mir zu hoch.

Der Gatte: Die Sache ist einfach die: wir haben vielleicht schon zehn oder zwölf Liebschaften miteinander gehabt ..... Kommt es dir nicht auch so vor?

5: The Married Lady and the Husband

A comfortable bedroom. Half past ten at night. The married lady is in bed, reading. The husband enters the room in dressing gown.

Married Lady: [Without looking up.] Not working anymore?
Husband: No. I'm too tired. And besides ...
Married Lady: What?
Husband: I suddenly felt so lonely sitting at my desk. I had a longing for you.

Married Lady: [Looking up.] Really?
Husband: [Sitting on the edge of the bed.] Don't read any more. You'll ruin your eyes.
Married Lady: [Closing the book.] Is anything wrong with you?
Husband: Nothing, dear. I'm just in love with you. You must know that!
Married Lady: There are times when one might forget it.
Husband: There are times when one should forget it.
Married Lady: Why?
Husband: Because otherwise marriage would be an imperfect thing. It would ... how shall I put it ... it would lose its sacredness.
Married Lady: Oh ...
Husband: Believe me ... that's true. If we hadn't sometimes forgotten ... during the five years we've been married ... that we were in love with each other − we certainly wouldn't be now.
Married Lady: That's over my head.
Husband: It's perfectly simple: we've had about ten or twelve love episodes together up to now, haven't we?

Die junge Frau: Ich hab' nicht gezählt! —

Der Gatte: Hätten wir gleich die erste bis zum Ende durchgekostet, hätte ich mich von Anfang an meiner Leidenschaft für dich willenlos hingegeben, es wäre uns gegangen wie den Millionen von anderen Liebespaaren. Wir wären fertig miteinander.

Die junge Frau: Ah .... so meinst du das?

Der Gatte: Glaube mir — Emma — in den ersten Tagen unserer Ehe hatte ich Angst, daß es so kommen würde.

Die junge Frau: Ich auch.

Der Gatte: Siehst du? Hab' ich nicht recht gehabt? Darum ist es gut, immer wieder für einige Zeit nur in guter Freundschaft miteinander hinzuleben.

Die junge Frau: Ach so.

Der Gatte: Und so kommt es, daß wir immer wieder neue Flitterwochen miteinander durchleben können, da ich es nie drauf ankommen lasse, die Flitterwochen ....

Die junge Frau: Zu Monaten auszudehnen.

Der Gatte: Richtig.

Die junge Frau: Und jetzt ...... scheint also wieder eine Freundschaftsperiode abgelaufen zu sein —?

Der Gatte: [sie zärtlich an sich drückend.] Es dürfte so sein.

Die junge Frau: Wenn es aber .... bei mir anders wäre.

Der Gatte: Es ist bei dir nicht anders. Du bist ja das klügste und entzückendste Wesen, das es gibt. Ich bin sehr glücklich, daß ich dich gefunden habe.

Die junge Frau: Das ist aber nett, wie du den Hof machen kannst — von Zeit zu Zeit.

Der Gatte: [hat sich auch zu Bett begeben.] Für einen Mann, der sich ein bischen in der Welt umgesehen hat — geh', leg den Kopf an meine Schulter — der sich in der Welt umgesehen hat, bedeutet die Ehe eigentlich etwas viel geheimnisvolleres als für euch junge Mädchen aus guter Familie. Ihr tretet uns rein und .... wenigstens bis zu einem gewissen Grad unwissend entgegen, und darum habt ihr eigentlich einen viel klareren Blick für das Wesen der Liebe als wir.

Die junge Frau: [lachend.] Oh!

Married Lady: I haven't counted!

Husband: If we'd drained the first one to the last drop, if I'd surrendered completely to my passion for you right at the start, the same thing that happens to millions of other loving couples would have happened to us. We'd be through with each other.

Married Lady: Oh ... that's what you mean!

Husband: Believe me, Emma — in the first days of our marriage I was afraid it would happen.

Married Lady: So was I.

Husband: You see? Wasn't I right? That's why it's such a wise thing from time to time to live together like good friends.

Married Lady: Oh, yes.

Husband: And that's why we're always able to live through our honeymoon days again, just because I never allow them to ...

Married Lady: Drag into months.

Husband: Quite so.

Married Lady: And now ... another period of friendship has apparently run its course.

Husband: [Pressing her to him tenderly.] So it seems.

Married Lady: But what if ... if I feel differently?

Husband: You don't feel differently. You're the wisest and most adorable creature that ever lived. I'm very happy that I've found you.

Married Lady: It's charming the way you can woo ... in sections.

Husband: [Slipping into bed.] To a man who's looked about the world a bit — come, lay your head on my shoulder — who's seen a bit of life, marriage seems much more mysterious, as a matter of fact, than it does to you girls of good family. You come to us pure ... and, up to a certain point, ignorant, and that's why you really have a much clearer insight into the way of love than we have.

Married Lady: [Laughing.] Oh!

Der Gatte: Gewiß. Denn wir sind ganz verwirrt und unsicher geworden durch die vielfachen Erlebnisse, die wir notgedrungen vor der Ehe durchzumachen haben. Ihr hört ja viel und wißt zu viel und lest ja wohl eigentlich auch zu viel, aber einen rechten Begriff von dem, was wir Männer in der Tat erleben, habt ihr ja doch nicht. Uns wird das, was man so gemeinhin die Liebe nennt, recht gründlich widerwärtig gemacht; denn was sind das schließlich für Geschöpfe, auf die wir angewiesen sind!

Die junge Frau: Ja, was sind das für Geschöpfe?

Der Gatte: [küßt sie auf die Stirn.] Sei froh, mein Kind, daß du nie einen Einblick in diese Verhältnisse erhalten hast. Es sind übrigens meist recht bedauernswerte Wesen — werfen wir keinen Stein auf sie.

Die junge Frau: Bitt' dich — dieses Mitleid — Das kommt mir da gar nicht recht angebracht vor.

Der Gatte: [mit schöner Milde.] Sie verdienen es. Ihr, die ihr junge Mädchen aus guter Familie wart, die ruhig unter Obhut euerer Eltern auf den Ehrenmann warten konntet, der euch zur Ehe begehrt; — ihr kennt ja das Elend nicht, das die meisten von diesen armen Geschöpfen der Sünde in die Arme treibt.

Die junge Frau: So verkaufen sich denn alle?

Der Gatte: Das möchte ich nicht sagen. Ich mein' ja auch nicht nur das materielle Elend. Aber es gibt auch — ich möchte sagen — ein sittliches Elend; eine mangelhafte Auffassung für das, was erlaubt, und insbesondere für das, was edel ist.

Die junge Frau: Aber warum sind die zu bedauern? — Denen geht's ja ganz gut?

Der Gatte: Du hast sonderbare Ansichten, mein Kind. Du darfst nicht vergessen, daß solche Wesen von Natur aus bestimmt sind, immer tiefer und tiefer zu fallen. Da gibt es kein Aufhalten.

Die junge Frau: [sich an ihn schmiegend.] Offenbar fällt es sich ganz angenehm.

Der Gatte: [peinlich berührt.] Wie kannst du so reden, Emma.

Husband: Certainly. Because all the varied experiences that we necessarily must pass through before marriage have confused and unsettled us. You've heard a lot and know a lot and have probably read a lot, but you have actually no conception of what we men have to live through. What is commonly called Love eventually becomes a thing utterly repellent to us; which is hardly surprising when you think of the creatures we have to turn to!

Married Lady: Tell me, what kind of creatures?

Husband: [Kissing her forehead.] Be thankful, my dear, that you've never had a glimpse of these conditions. Besides, most of these creatures are greatly to be pitied. We mustn't cast stones at them.

Married Lady: I think this pity of yours is a bit misplaced.

Husband: [With noble compassion.] They deserve it. You girls of refinement and good family, you who wait quietly under the protection of your parents for the honorable man who is to lead you into the bonds of matrimony — how can you know the misery that hounds these poor creatures into the arms of Sin?

Married Lady: But do they all sell themselves?

Husband: I wouldn't go so far as to say that. And I don't only mean material misery. There is also — I might say — a misery that is moral; an inability to grasp what is permissible, and more specifically, what is noble.

Married Lady: But why are they to be pitied? They get along quite well!

Husband: You have strange ideas, my dear. You mustn't forget that these creatures are destined by nature to sink lower and lower. There are no half-way stops for them.

Married Lady: [Cuddling up to him.] The sinking seems to be rather pleasurable.

Husband: [Pained.] How can you say things like that,

Ich denke doch, daß es gerade für euch, anständige Frauen, nichts Widerwärtigeres geben kann, als alle diejenigen, die es nicht sind.

Die junge Frau: Freilich, Karl, freilich. Ich hab's ja auch nur so gesagt. Geh', erzähl' weiter. Es ist so nett, wenn du so red'st. Erzähl' mir 'was.

Der Gatte: Was denn? —

Die junge Frau: Nun, — von diesen Geschöpfen.

Der Gatte: Was fällt dir denn ein?

Die junge Frau: Schau, ich hab' dich schon früher, weißt du, ganz im Anfang hab' ich dich immer gebeten, du sollst mir aus deiner Jugend 'was erzählen.

Der Gatte: Warum interessiert dich denn das?

Die junge Frau: Bist du denn nicht mein Mann? Und ist das nicht geradezu eine Ungerechtigkeit, daß ich von deiner Vergangenheit eigentlich gar nichts weiß? —

Der Gatte: Du wirst mich doch nicht für so geschmacklos halten, daß ich — Genug, Emma ...... das ist ja wie eine Entweihung.

Die junge Frau: Und doch hast du .... wer weiß wie viel andere Frauen gerade so in den Armen gehalten, wie jetzt mich.

Der Gatte: Sag' doch nicht »Frauen«. Frau bist du.

Die junge Frau: Aber eine Frage mußt du mir beantworten ... sonst .... sonst .... ist's nichts mit den Flitterwochen.

Der Gatte: Du hast eine Art, zu reden .... denk' doch, daß du Mutter bist .... daß unser Mäderl da drin liegt ...

Die junge Frau: [an ihn sich schmiegend.] Aber ich möcht' auch einen Buben.

Der Gatte: Emma!

Die junge Frau: Geh', sei nicht so ... freilich bin ich deine Frau .... aber ich möchte auch ein bissel .... deine Geliebte sein.

Der Gatte: Möchtest du?....

Die junge Frau: Also — zuerst meine Frage.

Der Gatte: [gefügig.] Nun?

Die junge Frau: War .... eine verheiratete Frau — unter ihnen?

Der Gatte: Wieso? — wie meinst du das?

Emma? I've always thought that nothing could be more repulsive to respectable women like you than those who are not respectable.

Married Lady: Oh, of course, Karl, of course. I was only talking. Go on, tell me some more. It's so nice when you speak like that. Tell me things.

Husband: What about?

Married Lady: Well — about these creatures.

Husband: Why on earth should I?

Married Lady: Look, Karl, don't you remember, I begged you right from the beginning, many times, to tell me things about your youth.

Husband: But why should that interest you?

Married Lady: Well, aren't you my husband? And isn't it unfair, my not knowing anything about your past? —

Husband: You surely don't expect me to be so tasteless as to — but enough, Emma ... that would be sacrilege.

Married Lady: And yet ... you must have held heaven knows how many other women in your arms like this.

Husband: Don't say "Women." You're the only "woman," to me.

Married Lady: But there's one question you've got to answer ... otherwise ... otherwise ... the honeymoon is out.

Husband: You certainly have a strange way of speaking ... remember that you're a mother ... that our little girl is sleeping right in there ...

Married Lady: [Cuddling again.] I'd like a little boy too.

Husband: Emma!

Married Lady: Oh, don't act like that ... certainly I'm your wife ... but I'd like to be your sweetheart too ... just a weeny bit.

Husband: Would you really?

Married Lady: Well — answer my question first.

Husband: Well?

Married Lady: Was ther ... a married woman ... among them?

Husband: What do you mean? What are you driving at?

Die junge Frau: Du weißt schon.

Der Gatte: [leicht beunruhigt.] Wie kommst du auf diese Frage?

Die junge Frau: Ich möchte wissen, ob es .... das heißt — es gibt solche Frauen .... das weiß ich. Aber ob du ...

Der Gatte: [ernst.] Kennst du eine solche Frau?

Die junge Frau: Ja, ich weiß das selber nicht.

Der Gatte: Ist unter deinen Freundinnen vielleicht eine solche Frau?

Die junge Frau: Ja wie kann ich das mit Bestimmtheit behaupten — oder verneinen?

Der Gatte: Hat dir vielleicht einmal eine deiner Freundinnen .... Man spricht über gar manches, wenn man so — die Frauen unter sich — hat dir eine gestanden —?

Die junge Frau: [unsicher.] Nein.

Der Gatte: Hast du bei irgend einer deiner Freundinnen den Verdacht, daß sie ....

Die junge Frau: Verdacht ..... oh ..... Verdacht.

Der Gatte: Es scheint.

Die junge Frau: Gewiß nicht Karl, sicher nicht. Wenn ich mir's so überlege — ich trau' es doch keiner zu.

Der Gatte: Keiner?

Die junge Frau: Von meinen Freundinnen keiner.

Der Gatte: Versprich mir etwas, Emma.

Die junge Frau: Nun.

Der Gatte: Daß du nie mit einer Frau verkehren wirst, bei der du auch den leisesten Verdacht hast, daß sie ...... kein ganz tadelloses Leben führt.

Die junge Frau: Das muß ich dir erst versprechen?

Der Gatte: Ich weiß ja, daß du den Verkehr mit solchen Frauen nicht suchen wirst. Aber der Zufall könnte es fügen, daß du ..... Ja, es ist sogar sehr häufig, daß gerade solche Frauen, deren Ruf nicht der beste ist, die Gesellschaft von anständigen Frauen suchen, teils um sich ein Relief zu geben, teils aus einem gewissen .... wie soll ich sagen ..... aus einem gewissen Heimweh nach der Tugend.

Die junge Frau: So.

Married Lady: You know perfectly well.

Husband: [Slightly disturbed.] What makes you ask that?

Married Lady: I'd like to know whether ... that is, I know there are women like that ... but I want to know whether you ...

Husband: [Serious.] Do you know a woman like that?

Married Lady: Well, I can't tell.

Husband: Do you suppose there's a woman like that among your friends?

Married Lady: How could I say, with certainty — or deny it?

Husband: Has one of your friends ever ... after all, when women are together they talk quite freely ... has one of them ever confessed ... ?

Married Lady: [Wavering.] No.

Husband: Have you ever suspected one of your friends of ...

Married Lady: Suspect ... Oh ... suspect ...

Husband: You seem to have.

Married Lady: Oh, no, Karl, absolutely not. When I think it over, I really couldn't imagine it of any one.

Husband: No one?

Married Lady: No one of my friends.

Husband: Promise me something, Emma.

Married Lady: Well?

Husband: That you'll never have anything to do with a woman who's the least bit under suspicion of not ... not leading a quite spotless life.

Married Lady: And I've got to promise you that now?

Husband: Of course I know that you won't try to associate with women like that. But it might just happen that you'd ... as a matter of fact, it occurs very often that just such women of doubtful reputation attach themselves to the society of decent women, partly to give themselves a foil, partly ... how shall I put it ... partly out of a sort of craving for virtue.

Married Lady: I see.

Der Gatte: Ja. Ich glaube, daß das sehr richtig ist, was ich da gesagt habe. Heimweh nach der Tugend. Denn, daß diese Frauen alle eigentlich sehr unglücklich sind, das kannst du mir glauben.

Die junge Frau: Warum?

Der Gatte: Du fragst, Emma? — Wie kannst du denn nur fragen? — Stell' dir doch vor, was diese Frauen für eine Existenz führen! Voll Lüge, Tücke, Gemeinheit und voll Gefahren.

Die junge Frau: Ja freilich. Da hast du schon Recht.

Der Gatte: Wahrhaftig — sie bezahlen das bischen Glück ..... das bischen .....

Die junge Frau: Vergnügen.

Der Gatte: Warum Vergnügen? Wie kommst du darauf, das Vergnügen zu nennen?

Die junge Frau: Nun, — etwas muß es doch sein —! Sonst täten sie's ja nicht.

Der Gatte: Nichts ist es ..... ein Rausch.

Die junge Frau: [nachdenklich.] Ein Rausch.

Der Gatte: Nein, es ist nicht einmal ein Rausch. Wie immer — teuer bezahlt, das ist gewiß!

Die junge Frau: Also ..... du hast das einmal mitgemacht — nicht wahr?

Der Gatte: Ja, Emma. — Es ist meine traurigste Erinnerung.

Die junge Frau: Wer ist's? Sag'! Kenn' ich sie?

Der Gatte: Was fällt dir denn ein?

Die junge Frau: Ist's lange her? War es sehr lang, bevor du mich geheiratet hast?

Der Gatte: Frag' nicht. Ich bitt' dich, frag' nicht.

Die junge Frau: Aber Karl!

Der Gatte: Sie ist tot.

Die junge Frau: Im Ernst?

Der Gatte: Ja ..... es klingt fast lächerlich, aber ich habe die Empfindung, daß alle diese Frauen jung sterben.

Die junge Frau: Hast du sie sehr geliebt?

Der Gatte: Lügnerinnen liebt man nicht.

Die junge Frau: Also warum ....

Der Gatte: Ein Rausch ....

Husband: Yes, I think I hit the nail on the head. Craving for virtue. For you may be sure that these women are all very unhappy.

Married Lady: Why?
Husband: You ask that, Emma? — How can you? Just imagine the kind of life these women lead! Full of lies, tricks, meanness, full of danger.

Married Lady: Yes, I suppose you're right.
Husband: Truly — they pay dearly for their crumb of happiness ... their crumb of ...
Married Lady: Pleasure.
Husband: Why pleasure? What makes you call that pleasure?

Married Lady: Well — there must be some —! Otherwise they wouldn't do it.
Husband: It's nothing at all ... just an intoxication.
Married Lady: [Reflectively.] An intoxication.
Husband: No, it isn't even intoxication. But whatever it is — it's dearly paid for, that's sure!
Married Lady: So you've ... you've been through it all once ... haven't you?
Husband: Yes, Emma. It's my saddest memory.
Married Lady: Who was it? Tell me! Do I know her?
Husband: Are you mad?
Married Lady: Was it long ago? Was it long before you married me?
Husband: Don't ask. I beg of you not to ask.
Married Lady: But, Karl!
Husband: She is dead.
Married Lady: You mean that?
Husband: It may sound a little ridiculous, but it strikes me that all these women die young.
Married Lady: Did you love her very much?
Husband: One doesn't love liars.
Married Lady: Then why ...
Husband: Intoxication.

Die junge Frau: Also doch?

Der Gatte: Sprich nicht mehr davon ich bitt' dich. Alles das ist lang vorbei. Geliebt hab' ich nur eine — das bist du. Man liebt nur, wo Reinheit und Wahrheit ist.

Die junge Frau: Karl!

Der Gatte: Oh, wie sicher, wie wohl fühlt man sich in solchen Armen. Warum hab' ich dich nicht schon als Kind gekannt? Ich glaube, dann hätt' ich andere Frauen überhaupt nicht angesehen.

Die junge Frau: Karl!

Der Gatte: Und schön bist du!.... schön!.... Oh komm' .... [Er löscht das Licht aus.]

*   *   *   *   *

Die junge Frau: Weißt du, woran ich heute denken muß?

Der Gatte: Woran, mein Schatz?

Die junge Frau: An .... an .... an Venedig.

Der Gatte: Die erste Nacht ....

Die junge Frau: Ja .... so ....

Der Gatte: Was denn —? So sag's doch!

Die junge Frau: So lieb hast du mich heut'.

Der Gatte: Ja, so lieb.

Die junge Frau: Ah .... Wenn du immer ....

Der Gatte: [in ihren Armen.] Wie?

Die junge Frau: Mein Karl!

Der Gatte: Was meintest du? Wenn ich immer ....

Die junge Frau: Nun ja.

Der Gatte: Nun, was wär' denn, wenn ich immer ...?

Die junge Frau: Dann wüßt' ich eben immer, daß du mich lieb hast.

Der Gatte: Ja. Du mußt es aber auch so wissen. Man ist nicht immer der liebende Mann, man muß auch zuweilen hinaus ins feindliche Leben, muß kämpfen und streben! Das vergiß nie, mein Kind! Alles hat seine Zeit in der Ehe — das ist eben das Schöne. Es gibt nicht viele, die sich noch nach fünf Jahren an — ihr Venedig erinnern.

Die junge Frau: Freilich!

Der Gatte: Und jetzt .... gute Nacht, mein Kind.

Die junge Frau: Gute Nacht!

Married Lady: So it is that, after all?

Husband: Don't talk about it any more, please. All that is long past. There's only one I've ever loved — and that's you. One can only love where one finds purity and truth.

Married Lady: Karl!

Husband: Oh, how safe, how wonderful one feels in arms like yours. Why didn't I know you when you were a child? Then I think I wouldn't even have looked at other women.

Married Lady: Karl!

Husband: How beautiful you are! Beautiful! Oh, come ... [Turns out the light.]

* * * * *

Married Lady: Do you know what this reminds me of?

Husband: What, my darling?

Married Lady: Of ... of ... of Venice.

Husband: The first night ...

Married Lady: Yes ... you ...

Husband: What? Come, tell me!

Married Lady: You — you're just as in love.

Husband: Yes.

Married Lady: Oh ... if only you'd always ...

Husband: [In her arms.] If what?

Married Lady: My own Karl!

Husband: What did you mean, if only I'd always ... ?

Married Lady: Oh, well ...

Husband: Come, what was that, if only I'd always ...

Married Lady: Well then, I'd always know that you loved me.

Husband: You should know that anyway. One can't always be the lover, one has to enter the battle of life now and then, to fight and struggle! Don't ever forget that, my dear. There's time for everything in married life — that's the beautiful part of it. There aren't many who — after five years — can still remember Venice.

Married Lady: Oh, no!

Husband: And now ... good night, my dearest!

Married Lady: Good night!

6: Der Gatte und das süsse Mädel

Ein Kabinet particulier im Riedhof. Behagliche, mäßige Eleganz. Der Gasofen brennt. Auf dem Tisch sind die Reste einer Mahlzeit zu sehen; Obersschaumbaisers, Obst, Käse. In den Weingläsern ein ungarischer weißer Wein.

Der Gatte raucht eine Havannazigarre, er lehnt in der Ecke des Divans.

Das süsse Mädel sitzt neben ihm auf dem Sessel und löffelt aus einem Baiser den Obersschaum heraus, den sie mit Behagen schlürft.

Der Gatte: Schmeckt's?

Das süsse Mädel: [läßt sich nicht stören.] Oh!

Der Gatte: Willst du noch eins?

Das süsse Mädel: Nein, ich hab' so schon zu viel gegessen.

Der Gatte: Du hast keinen Wein mehr. [Er schenkt ein.]

Das süsse Mädel: Nein .... aber schaun' S', ich laß ihn ja eh stehen.

Der Gatte: Komm setz' dich zu mir.

Das süsse Mädel: Gleich .... bin noch nicht fertig. [Der Gatte steht auf, stellt sich hinter den Sessel und umarmt daß süße Mädel, indem er ihren Kopf zu sich wendet.] Na, was ist denn?

Der Gatte: Einen Kuß möcht' ich haben.

Das süsse Mädel: [giebt ihm einen Kuß.] Sie sind .... oh pardon, du bist ein kecker Mensch.

Der Gatte: Jetzt fällt dir das ein?

Das süsse Mädel: Ah nein, eingefallen ist es mir schon früher .... schon auf der Gassen. Du mußt dir eigentlich was schönes von mir denken.

Der Gatte: Warum denn?

6: The Husband and the Sweet Young Girl

A private room in the Restaurant Riedhof, comfortable, moderately elegant. The gas oven is lit. The remnants of a meal are on the table. Pastry, fruit, cheese. A Hungarian white wine is in the wine glasses.

The husband is smoking an Havana cigar and leaning back in a corner of the sofa.

The sweet young girl sits on a chair next to him and, with a spoon, scoops off the whipped cream from the pastry, swallowing it with pleasure.

Husband: Taste good?
Sweet Young Girl: [Eats on.] Oh!
Husband: Want another?
Sweet Young Girl: No, I've eaten too much already.
Husband: You haven't any wine left. [Fills her glass.]
Sweet Young Girl: No ... please ... I'll just let it stand.

Husband: Come, sit by me.
Sweet Young Girl: Just a minute ... not finished yet. [Husband stands up, goes behind her chair and puts his arms around her, turning her head up to him.] Well, what is it?
Husband: I'd like a kiss.
Sweet Young Girl: [Gives him a kiss.] You're pretty fresh.

Husband: Has that just occurred to you?
Sweet Young Girl: Oh, no, I discovered that before ... on the street. You must have a fine opinion of me.

Husband: Why?

Das süsse Mädel: Daß ich gleich so mit Ihnen ins chambre separée gegangen bin.

Der Gatte: Na, gleich kann man doch nicht sagen.

Das süsse Mädel: Aber Sie können halt so schön bitten.

Der Gatte: Findest du?

Das süsse Mädel: Und schließlich, was ist denn dabei?

Der Gatte: Freilich.

Das süsse Mädel: Ob man spazieren geht oder −

Der Gatte: Zum spazieren gehen ist es auch viel zu kalt.

Das süsse Mädel: Natürlich ist zu kalt gewesen.

Der Gatte: Aber da ist es angenehm warm; was? [Er hat sich wieder niedergesetzt, umschlingt das süße Mädel und zieht sie an seine Seite.]

Das süsse Mädel: [schwach.] Na.

Der Gatte: Jetzt sag' einmal .... Du hast mich schon früher bemerkt gehabt, was?

Das süsse Mädel: Natürlich. Schon in der Singerstraßen.

Der Gatte: Nicht heut, mein' ich. Auch vorgestern und vorvorgestern, wie ich dir nachgegangen bin.

Das süsse Mädel: Mir geh'n gar viele nach.

Der Gatte: Das kann ich mir denken. Aber ob du mich bemerkt hast.

Das süsse Mädel: Wissen S' .... ah .... weißt, was mir neulich passiert ist? Da ist mir der Mann von meiner Cousine nachg'stiegen in der Dunkeln und hat mich nicht 'kennt.

Der Gatte: Hat er dich angesprochen?

Das süsse Mädel: Aber was glaubst denn? Meinst, es ist jeder so keck wie du?

Der Gatte: Aber es kommt doch vor.

Das süsse Mädel: Natürlich kommt's vor.

Der Gatte: Na, was machst du da?

Das süsse Mädel: Na, nichts − Keine Antwort geb' ich halt.

Der Gatte: Hm .... mir hast du aber eine Antwort gegeben.

Das süsse Mädel: Na sind S' vielleicht bös'?

Der Gatte: [küßt sie heftig.] Deine Lippen schmecken nach dem Obersschaum.

Das süsse Mädel: Oh, die sind von Natur aus süß.

Sweet Young Girl: For going to a private room with you right away.

Husband: Well, hardly right away.

Sweet Young Girl: But you do have such a winning way.

Husband: Think so, really?

Sweet Young Girl: And after all, what's the harm?

Husband: What indeed.

Sweet Young Girl: What difference is it whether one goes for a walk or —

Husband: It's too cold to walk, anyway.

Sweet Young Girl: Oh, much too cold.

Husband: But it's nice and warm here, isn't it? [Sits on the sofa again, pulling the Sweet young girl down next to him.]

Sweet Young Girl: [Weakening.] Yes ...

Husband: Tell me ... you've noticed me before, haven't you?

Sweet Young Girl: Of course. I noticed you on Singer Street.

Husband: I don't mean only today. I mean the day before, and the day before that, when I was following you.

Sweet Young Girl: Lots of men follow me.

Husband: I don't doubt it. But did you notice me?

Sweet Young Girl: Do you know what happened to me just the other day? My own cousin's husband tried to follow me in the dark and didn't recognize me.

Husband: Did he speak to you?

Sweet Young Girl: Speak to me? D'you think everybody's as fresh as you are?

Husband: Well, it does happen, you know.

Sweet Young Girl: Certainly it happens.

Husband: Well what do you do then?

Sweet Young Girl: Nothing at all. I just don't answer.

Husband: Hmmm ... but you answered me.

Sweet Young Girl: Are you mad at me?

Husband: [Kissing her impulsively.] Your lips taste of whipped cream.

Sweet Young Girl: Oh, they're naturally sweet.

Der Gatte: Das haben dir schon viele gesagt?

Das süsse Mädel: Viele!! Was du dir wieder einbildest!

Der Gatte: Na, sei einmal ehrlich. Wie viele haben den Mund da schon geküßt?

Das süsse Mädel: Was fragst mich denn? Du möcht'st mir's ja doch nicht glauben, wenn ich dir's sag'!

Der Gatte: Warum denn nicht?

Das süsse Mädel: Rat' einmal.

Der Gatte: Na, sagen wir, — aber du darfst nicht bös' sein?

Das süsse Mädel: Warum sollt' ich denn bös' sein?

Der Gatte: Also ich schätze .... zwanzig.

Das süsse Mädel: [sich von ihm losmachend.] Na — warum nicht gleich hundert?

Der Gatte: Ja, ich hab' eben geraten.

Das süsse Mädel: Da hast du aber nicht gut geraten.

Der Gatte: Also zehn.

Das süsse Mädel: [beleidigt.] Freilich. Eine, die sich auf der Gassen anreden läßt und gleich mitgeht ins chambre separée!

Der Gatte: Sei doch nicht so kindisch. Ob man auf der Straßen herumläuft oder in einem Zimmer sitzt .... Wir sind doch da in einem Gasthaus. Jeden Moment kann der Kellner hereinkommen — da ist doch wirklich gar nichts dran ....

Das süsse Mädel: Das hab' ich mir eben auch gedacht.

Der Gatte: Warst du schon einmal in einem chambre separée?

Das süsse Mädel: Also, wenn ich die Wahrheit sagen soll: ja.

Der Gatte: Siehst du, das g'fallt mir, daß du doch wenigstens aufrichtig bist.

Das süsse Mädel: Aber nicht so — wie du dir's wieder denkst. Mit einer Freundin und ihrem Bräutigam bin ich im chambre separée gewesen, heuer im Fasching einmal.

Der Gatte: Es wär' ja auch kein Malheur, wenn du einmal — mit deinem Geliebten —

Das süsse Mädel: Natürlich wär's kein Malheur. Aber ich hab' kein' Geliebten.

Der Gatte: Na geh'.

Das süsse Mädel: Meiner Seel', ich hab' keinen.

Husband: I suppose a great many have told you that?

Sweet Young Girl: A great many! What crazy ideas you have!

Husband: Be honest for once. How many have kissed this mouth of yours?

Sweet Young Girl: Why do you want to know? You wouldn't believe it if I told you!

Husband: Why not?

Sweet Young Girl: Try and guess.

Husband: Well ... let's say ... but you won't be angry?

Sweet Young Girl: Why should I be angry?

Husband: Alright then, I guess ... twenty.

Sweet Young Girl: [Freeing herself from him.] Why not start at a hundred?

Husband: Well, I only guessed.

Sweet Young Girl: But you didn't guess right.

Husband: Alright, then, ten.

Sweet Young Girl: [Offended.] Of course. When a girl lets herself get talked to on the street and goes right to a private room with a man ...

Husband: Don't be so childish. Whether one walks along the street or sits in a room ... After all, we're in a restaurant. Any moment the waiter might come in — there's really nothing wrong in it ...

Sweet Young Girl: That's what I just figured out myself.

Husband: Were you ever in a private room before?

Sweet Young Girl: Well, if I must speak the truth; yes.

Husband: Now, I like it when you're straightforward like that.

Sweet Young Girl: But not the way — the way you think. I was in a private room with a girl friend and her fiancé last Easter, once.

Husband: It wouldn't have been a catastrophe if you'd gone once with — your sweetheart.

Sweet Young Girl: Of course it wouldn't have been a catastrophe. But I have no sweetheart.

Husband: Oh, go on!

Sweet Young Girl: Honest to God I haven't.

Der Gatte: Aber du wirst mir doch nicht einreden wollen, daß ich ....

Das süsse Mädel: Was denn?.... Ich hab' halt keinen — schon seit mehr als einem halben Jahr.

Der Gatte: Ah so .... Aber vorher? Wer war's denn?

Das süsse Mädel: Was sind S' denn gar so neugierig?

Der Gatte: Ich bin neugierig, weil ich dich lieb hab'.

Das süsse Mädel: Is wahr?

Der Gatte: Freilich. Das mußt du doch merken. Erzähl' mir also. [Drückt sie fest an sich.]

Das süsse Mädel: Was soll ich dir denn erzählen?

Der Gatte: So laß dich doch nicht so lang bitten. Wer's gewesen ist, möcht ich wissen.

Das süsse Mädel: [lachend.] Na ein Mann halt.

Der Gatte: Also — also — wer war's?

Das süsse Mädel: Ein bissel ähnlich hat er dir gesehen.

Der Gatte: So.

Das süsse Mädel: Wenn du ihm nicht so ähnlich schauen tät'st —

Der Gatte: Was wär' dann?

Das süsse Mädel: Na also frag' nicht, wennst schon siehst, daß ....

Der Gatte: [versteht.] Also darum hast du dich von mir anreden lassen.

Das süsse Mädel: Na also ja.

Der Gatte: Jetzt weiß ich wirklich nicht, soll ich mich freuen oder soll ich mich ärgern.

Das süsse Mädel: Na, ich an deiner Stell' tät' mich freuen.

Der Gatte: Na ja.

Das süsse Mädel: Und auch im Reden erinnerst du mich so an ihn .... und wie du einen anschaust ....

Der Gatte: Was ist er denn gewesen?

Das süsse Mädel: Nein, die Augen —

Der Gatte: Wie hat er denn geheißen?

Das süsse Mädel: Nein, schau mich nicht so an, ich bitt' dich. [Der Gatte umfängt sie. Langer, heißer Kuß. Das süsse Mädel schüttelt sich, will aufstehen.]

Der Gatte: Warum gehst du fort von mir?

Husband: But you're not trying to make me believe that I'm ...

Sweet Young Girl: That you what? ... I haven't had one for over six months.

Husband: Oh, I see ... But before that? Who was it then?

Sweet Young Girl: Why are you so curious?

Husband: I'm curious because I love you.

Sweet Young Girl: Do you mean that?

Husband: Of course I do. You must see that. So come, tell me. [Presses her closely to him.]

Sweet Young Girl: Well, what do you want me to tell you?

Husband: Oh, don't make me go on coaxing you. I want to know who it was.

Sweet Young Girl: [Laughing.] Well, a man.

Husband: But who — who?

Sweet Young Girl: He looked a little like you.

Husband: Did he now?

Sweet Young Girl: If you hadn't looked so much like him ...

Husband: What would have happened?

Sweet Young Girl: Now why ask, when you see that ...

Husband: [Understanding.] Oh, so that's why you let me speak to you.

Sweet Young Girl: Yes, if you insist.

Husband: Now I really don't know whether to be glad or annoyed.

Sweet Young Girl: I'd be glad if I were in your place.

Husband: I suppose so.

Sweet Young Girl: Even the way you talk reminds me so of him ... and the way you look at one ...

Husband: What was he?

Sweet Young Girl: Even the eyes —

Husband: What was his name?

Sweet Young Girl: Don't look at me that way, please. [Husband embraces her. Long, passionate kiss. Sweet young girl tries to pull herself free and stand up.]

Husband: Why do you go away from me?

Das süsse Mädel: Es wird Zeit zum Z'haus'geh'n.

Der Gatte: Später.

Das süsse Mädel: Nein, ich muß wirklich schon zuhaus' gehen. Was glaubst denn, was die Mutter sagen wird.

Der Gatte: Du wohnst bei deiner Mutter?

Das süsse Mädel: Natürlich wohn' ich bei meiner Mutter. Was hast denn geglaubt?

Der Gatte: So — bei der Mutter. Wohnst du allein mit ihr?

Das süsse Mädel: Ja freilich allein! Fünf sind wir! Zwei Buben und noch zwei Mädeln.

Der Gatte: So setz' dich doch nicht so weit fort von mir. Bist du die älteste?

Das süsse Mädel: Nein, ich bin die zweite. Zuerst kommt die Kathi; die ist im G'schäft, in einer Blumenhandlung, dann komm' ich.

Der Gatte: Wo bist du?

Das süsse Mädel: Na ich bin z'haus'.

Der Gatte: Immer?

Das süsse Mädel: Es muß doch eine z'haus' sein.

Der Gatte: Freilich. Ja, — und was sagst du denn eigentlich deiner Mutter, wenn du — so spät nach Haus' kommst?

Das süsse Mädel: Das ist ja so eine Seltenheit.

Der Gatte: Also heut' zum Beispiel. Deine Mutter fragt dich doch?

Das süsse Mädel: Natürlich fragt s' mich. Da kann ich Obacht geben so viel ich will — wenn ich nach Haus' komm', wacht s' auf.

Der Gatte: Also was sagst du ihr da?

Das süsse Mädel: Na, im Theater werd' ich halt gewesen sein.

Der Gatte: Und glaubt sie das?

Das süsse Mädel: Na, warum soll s' mir denn nicht glauben? Ich geh' ja oft ins Theater. Erst am Sonntag war ich in der Oper mit meiner Freundin und ihrem Bräutigam und mein' älter'n Bruder.

Der Gatte: Woher habt ihr denn da die Karten?

Das süsse Mädel: Aber, mein Bruder ist ja Friseur.

Der Gatte: Ja, die Friseure ...... ah, wahrscheinlich Theaterfriseur.

Sweet Young Girl: It's time to go home.

Husband: Later.

Sweet Young Girl: No, really I must go home now. What do you suppose mother would say?

Husband: You live with your mother?

Sweet Young Girl: Of course I live with my mother. What did you think?

Husband: I see. Do you live alone with her?

Sweet Young Girl: "Alone" is good! There're five of us! Two boys and two more girls.

Husband: Don't sit so far away from me. Are you the oldest?

Sweet Young Girl: No, I'm the second. The oldest is Kathi, she's in business, in a flower-shop. Then I come.

Husband: And what do you do?

Sweet Young Girl: Me? I stay home.

Husband: All the time?

Sweet Young Girl: Well, someone's got to stay home.

Husband: Yes, of course — but what do you say to your mother when you — come home very late?

Sweet Young Girl: That happens very seldom.

Husband: Well, today, for instance. Your mother'll ask you, won't she?

Sweet Young Girl: Certainly she'll ask me. No matter how careful I am, they all wake up when I come in.

Husband: Well, what will you say to her?

Sweet Young Girl: I'll say I've been to the theatre.

Husband: Will she believe that?

Sweet Young Girl: Why shouldn't she? I go to the theatre lots. Why, just last Sunday I was at the opera with my girlfriend and her fiancé and my older brother.

Husband: Where do you get the tickets?

Sweet Young Girl: Oh, my brother's a hairdresser!

Husband: Ah, hairdressers ... probably theatrical hairdresser.

Das süsse Mädel: Was fragst mich denn so aus?

Der Gatte: Es interessiert mich halt. Und was ist denn der andere Bruder?

Das süsse Mädel: Der geht noch in die Schul'. Der will ein Lehrer werden. Nein .... so 'was!

Der Gatte: Und dann hast du noch eine kleine Schwester?

Das süsse Mädel: Ja, die ist noch ein Fratz, aber auf die muß man schon heut' so aufpassen. Hast du denn eine Idee, wie die Mädeln in der Schule verdorben werden! Was glaubst! Neulich hab' ich sie bei einem Rendezvous erwischt.

Der Gatte: Was?

Das süsse Mädel: Ja! mit einem Buben von der Schul vis-à-vis ist sie Abends um halber acht in der Strozzigasse spazieren gegangen. So ein Fratz!

Der Gatte: Und, was hast du da gemacht?

Das süsse Mädel: Na, Schläg' hat s' kriegt!

Der Gatte: So streng bist du?

Das süsse Mädel: Na, wer soll's denn sein? Die ältere ist im G'schäft, die Mutter tut nichts als raunzen; — kommt immer alles auf mich.

Der Gatte: Herrgott, bist du lieb! [Küßt sie und wird zärtlicher.] Du erinnerst mich auch an wen.

Das süsse Mädel: So — an wen denn?

Der Gatte: An keine bestimmte .... an die Zeit .... na, halt an meine Jugend. Geh, trink', mein Kind!

Das süsse Mädel: Ja, wie alt bist du denn?.... Du .... ja ... ich weiß ja nicht einmal, wie du heißt.

Der Gatte: Karl.

Das süsse Mädel: Ist's möglich! Karl heißt du?

Der Gatte: Er hat auch Karl geheißen?

Das süsse Mädel: Nein, das ist aber schon das reine Wunder ... das ist ja — nein die Augen .... Das G'schau .... [schüttelt den Kopf.]

Der Gatte: Und wer er war — hast du mir noch immer nicht gesagt.

Das süsse Mädel: Ein schlechter Mensch ist er gewesen — das ist g'wiß, sonst hätt' er mich nicht sitzen lassen.

Sweet Young Girl: Why are you so curious?
Husband: It interests me. And what is your other brother?

Sweet Young Girl: He's still in school. He wants to be a
    teacher. Did you ever!
Husband: And then you have a little sister besides?
Sweet Young Girl: Yes, she's still a kid, but you've got to keep
    an eye on her already. You have know idea how bad
    girls get in school nowadays! Would you believe it, I
    caught her having a rendezvous the other day.

Husband: Really?
Sweet Young Girl: Yes. She went walking with a boy from the
    school at half past seven, in Strozzi Lane. The little brat!

Husband: What did you do?
Sweet Young Girl: I gave her a spanking, alright!
Husband: You're strict, aren't you?
Sweet Young Girl: Who else is there to be? The oldest girl is in
    business and all mother does is nag. Everything always
    falls on me.
Husband: God, but you're sweet! [Kisses her, grows tender
    again.] You remind me of somebody too.
Sweet Young Girl: Really? Who?
Husband: Not anyone special ... just the ... oh, well, when I
    was young. Come, my child, drink!
Sweet Young Girl: How old are you, anyway? ... You ... oh,
    dear ... I don't even know what your name is.
Husband: Karl.
Sweet Young Girl: Is it really? You're really called Karl?
Husband: Was his name Karl, too?
Sweet Young Girl: No, that's absolutely a miracle ... that's ...
    and the eyes ... the expression ... [Shakes her head.]

Husband: But you haven't yet told me who he was.

Sweet Young Girl: He was a rotter, that's what he was — or
    else he wouldn't have left me in the lurch.

Der Gatte: Hast ihn sehr gern g'habt?

Das süsse Mädel: Freilich hab' ich ihn gern g'habt!

Der Gatte: Ich weiß, was er war, Lieutenant.

Das süsse Mädel: Nein, bei Militär war er nicht. Sie haben ihn nicht genommen. Sein Vater hat ein Haus in der .... aber was brauchst du das zu wissen?

Der Gatte: [küßt sie.] Du hast eigentlich graue Augen, anfangs hab' ich gemeint sie sind schwarz.

Das süsse Mädel: Na sind s' dir vielleicht nicht schön genug? [Der Gatte küßt ihre Augen.] Nein nein — das vertrag' ich schon gar nicht .... oh bitt' dich — oh Gott .... nein, laß mich aufsteh'n .... nur für einen Moment — bitt' dich.

Der Gatte: [immer zärtlicher.] Oh nein.

Das süsse Mädel: Aber ich bitt' dich, Karl ....

Der Gatte: Wie alt bist du? — achtzehn, was?

Das süsse Mädel: Neunzehn vorbei.

Der Gatte: Neunzehn .... und ich —

Das süsse Mädel: Du bist dreißig ....

Der Gatte: Und einige drüber. — Reden wir nicht davon.

Das süsse Mädel: Er war auch schon zweiundreißig, wie ich ihn kennen gelernt hab'.

Der Gatte: Wie lang ist das her?

Das süsse Mädel: Ich weiß nimmer .... Du, in dem Wein muß 'was d'rin gewesen sein.

Der Gatte: Ja, warum denn?

Das süsse Mädel: Ich bin ganz .... weißt — mir dreht sich alles.

Der Gatte: So halt' dich fest an mich. So .... [Er drückt sie an sich und wird immer zärtlicher, sie wehrt kaum ab.] Ich werd' dir 'was sagen, mein Schatz, wir könnten jetzt wirklich geh'n.

Das süsse Mädel: Ja .... nach Haus.

Der Gatte: Nicht g'rad' nach Haus .....

Das süsse Mädel: Was meinst denn?... Oh nein, oh nein ... ich geh' nirgends hin, was fallt dir denn ein —

Der Gatte: Also hör' mich nur an, mein Kind, das nächste Mal, wenn wir uns treffen, weißt du, da richten wir uns

Husband: Did you love him very much?

Sweet Young Girl: Certainly I did.

Husband: I know what he was, a lieutenant.

Sweet Young Girl: No, he wasn't in the army. They didn't take him. His father has a house in ... but why should you know that?

Husband: [Kissing her.] You've got grey eyes ... at first I thought they were black.

Sweet Young Girl: Well, aren't they pretty enough for you? [Husband kisses her eyes.] No, no ... that's more than I can stand ... please ... Oh, Lord ... no, please, let me get up ... just for a minute ... please.

Husband: [More and more caressing.] Oh, no.

Sweet Young Girl: Please, Karl ...

Husband: How old are you? Eighteen?

Sweet Young Girl: Past nineteen.

Husband: Nineteen ... and I —

Sweet Young Girl: You're thirty ...

Husband: And then some ... Don't let's talk about it.

Sweet Young Girl: He was thirty-two, too, when I met him.

Husband: How long ago was that.

Sweet Young Girl: I don't remember anymore ... Say, there must have been something in my wine.

Husband: Why?

Sweet Young Girl: I'm all ... everything swims around ...

Husband: Just hold on to me tight. That's right ... [He presses her to him, becomes more and more affectionate. She hardly resists him.] Listen, my sweet, we might just as well go now.

Sweet Young Girl: Yes ... home.

Husband: No, not exactly home ...

Sweet Young Girl: What do you mean? ... Oh, no; oh, no ... I won't go anywhere, how can you suggest —

Husband: Well then, my dear, listen — next time we meet we'll arrange it so that ... [He has slipped to the floor,

das so ein, daß ... [Er ist zu Boden gesunken, hat seinen Kopf in ihrem Schoß.] Das ist angenehm, oh, das ist angenehm.

Das süsse Mädel: Was machst denn? [Sie küßt seine Haare.] .... Du in dem Wein muß 'was drin gewesen sein — so schläfrig .... du, was g'schieht denn, wenn ich nimmer aufsteh'n kann? Aber, aber, schau, aber Karl .... und wenn wer hereinkommt .... ich bitt' dich .... der Kellner.

Der Gatte: Da .... kommt sein Lebtag .... kein Kellner .... herein ....

* * * * *

[Das süsse Mädel lehnt mit geschlossenen Augen in der Divanecke. Der Gatte geht in dem kleinen Raum auf und ab, nachdem er sich eine Zigarette angezündet. Längeres Schweigen.]

Der Gatte: [betrachtet das süße Mädel lange, für sich.] Wer weiß, was das eigentlich für eine Person ist — Donnerwetter .... So schnell .... War nicht sehr vorsichtig von mir .... Hm ....

Das süsse Mädel: [ohne die Augen zu öffnen.] In dem Wein muß 'was d'rin gewesen sein.

Der Gatte: Ja warum denn?

Das süsse Mädel: Sonst ....

Der Gatte: Warum schiebst du denn alles auf den Wein? ....

Das süsse Mädel: Wo bist denn? Warum bist denn so weit? Komm' doch zu mir. [Der Gatte zu ihr hin, setzt sich.] Jetzt sag' mir, ob du mich wirklich gern hast.

Der Gatte: Das weißt du doch .... [Er unterbricht sich rasch.] Freilich.

Das süsse Mädel: Weißt .... es ist doch .... Geh', sag' mir die Wahrheit, was war in dem Wein?

Der Gatte: Ja, glaubst du ich bin ein .... ich bin ein Giftmischer?

Das süsse Mädel: Ja, schau, ich versteh's halt nicht. Ich bin doch nicht so .... Wir kennen uns doch erst seit .... Du, ich bin nicht so .... meiner Seel' und Gott, — wenn du das von mir glauben tät'st —

Der Gatte: Ja — was machst du dir denn da für Sorgen. Ich

and laid his head in her lap.] That's lovely, oh, that's
lovely ...

Sweet Young Girl: What are you doing? [Kisses his hair.]
Listen, there must have been something in that wine ...
so sleepy ... what'd happen if I couldn't get up again?
But, Karl, listen ... Karl, really ... if someone should
come in ... please, Karl ... the waiter ...

Husband: Not a chance ... no waiter will come in here ... not
if I know it ...

* * * * *

[Sweet young girl leans against the corner of the sofa with
closed eyes. Husband paces to and fro in the small
room, then lights a cigarette. Prolonged silence.]

Husband: [Contemplating the Sweet young girl for a long
time, to himself.] Who knows who this girl really is,
anyway? ... Damn it all ... So quick ... not very wise of
me ... Hmmm ...

Sweet Young Girl: [Without opening her eyes.] There must
have been something in the wine.

Husband: But why?

Sweet Young Girl: Otherwise ...

Husband: Why do you blame everything on the wine? ...

Sweet Young Girl: Where are you? Why are you so far away?
Come to me. [Husband goes and sits next to her.] Now
tell me, do you really like me?

Husband: You know I do ... [Stops short.] Of course I do.

Sweet Young Girl: But, honest ... it's so ... Come on, tell me the
truth, what was in the wine?

Husband: What do you think I am, a poisoner?

Sweet Young Girl: But, look, I don't understand. I'm really
not so ... After all, we've only known each other for
... Honest, I'm not like this ... Honest to God — if you
thought that of me ...

Husband: What are you worrying about? I don't think

glaub' gar nichts schlechtes von dir. Ich glaub' halt, daß du mich lieb hast.

Das süsse Mädel: Ja ....

Der Gatte: Schließlich, wenn zwei junge Leut' allein in einem Zimmer sind, und nachtmahlen und trinken Wein .... es braucht gar nichts d'rin zu sein in dem Wein.

Das süsse Mädel: Ich hab's ja auch nur so g'sagt.

Der Gatte: Ja warum denn?

Das süsse Mädel: [eher trotzig.] Ich hab' mich halt g'schämt.

Der Gatte: Das ist lächerlich. Dazu liegt gar kein Grund vor. Umsomehr als ich dich an deinen ersten Geliebten erinnere.

Das süsse Mädel: Ja.

Der Gatte: An den ersten.

Das süsse Mädel: Na ja ....

Der Gatte: Jetzt möcht' es mich interessieren, wer die anderen waren.

Das süsse Mädel: Niemand.

Der Gatte: Das ist ja nicht wahr, das kann ja nicht wahr sein.

Das süsse Mädel: Geh' bitt' dich, sekier' mich nicht. —

Der Gatte: Willst eine Zigarette?

Das süsse Mädel: Nein, ich dank' schön.

Der Gatte: Weißt du, wie spät es ist?

Das süsse Mädel: Na?

Der Gatte: Halb zwölf.

Das süsse Mädel: So!

Der Gatte: Na .... und die Mutter? Die ist es gewöhnt, was?

Das süsse Mädel: Willst mich wirklich schon z'haus schicken?

Der Gatte: Ja, du hast doch früher selbst —

Das süsse Mädel: Geh', du bist aber wie ausgewechselt. Was hab' ich dir denn getan?

Der Gatte: Aber Kind, was hast du denn, was fällt dir denn ein?

Das süsse Mädel: Und es ist nur dein G'schau gewesen, meiner Seel', sonst hätt'st du lang .... haben mich schon viele gebeten, ich soll mit ihnen ins chambre separée gehen.

anything bad about you. I just think that you're fond of me.

Sweet Young Girl: Yes ...

Husband: After all, when two young people are alone in a room together eating supper and drinking wine ... there doesn't have to be anything in the wine.

Sweet Young Girl: Oh, I didn't really mean that.

Husband: Then what did you say it for?

Sweet Young Girl: [Rather defiantly.] I was ashamed of myself.

Husband: That's absurd. There's absolutely no reason for that. Especially since I remind you of your first love.

Sweet Young Girl: Yes.

Husband: Of the first.

Sweet Young Girl: Yes, that's right.

Husband: Now I'd like very much to know who the others were.

Sweet Young Girl: There weren't any.

Husband: That's not true; that can't be true.

Sweet Young Girl: Please stop nagging at me. —

Husband: Want a cigarette?

Sweet Young Girl: No, thanks.

Husband: Do you know how late it is?

Sweet Young Girl: No, what?

Husband: Half past eleven.

Sweet Young Girl: Really?

Husband: Well — but — how about your mother? She's used to it, is she?

Sweet Young Girl: Do you really want to send me home already?

Husband: But a while ago you yourself —

Sweet Young Girl: You've changed, haven't you? What did I do to you?

Husband: Don't be silly, child, nothing of the kind.

Sweet Young Girl: Honest to God, it was only your expression that did it, otherwise I'd have been ... long ago ... lots of men have begged me to go to a private room with them.

Der Gatte: Na, willst du .... bald wieder mit mir hieher .... oder auch wo anders —

Das süsse Mädel: Weiß nicht.

Der Gatte: Was heißt das wieder: Du weißt nicht.

Das süsse Mädel: Na, wenn du mich erst fragst?

Der Gatte: Also wann? Ich möcht' dich nur vor allem aufklären, daß ich nicht in Wien lebe. Ich komm' nur von Zeit zu Zeit auf ein paar Tage her.

Das süsse Mädel: Ah geh', du bist kein Wiener?

Der Gatte: Wiener bin ich schon. Aber ich lebe jetzt in der Nähe ....

Das süsse Mädel: Wo denn?

Der Gatte: Ach Gott, das ist ja egal.

Das süsse Mädel: Na, fürcht' dich nicht, ich komm' nicht hin.

Der Gatte: Oh Gott, wenn es dir Spaß macht, kannst du auch hinkommen. Ich lebe in Graz.

Das süsse Mädel: Du bist verheiratet, wie?

Der Gatte: [höchst erstaunt.] Ja, wie kommst du darauf?

Das süsse Mädel: Mir ist halt so vorgekommen.

Der Gatte: Und das würde dich gar nicht genieren?

Das süsse Mädel: Na, lieber ist mir schon, du bist ledig. — Aber du bist ja doch verheiratet! —

Der Gatte: Ja, sag' mir nur, wie kommst du denn da darauf?

Das süsse Mädel: Wenn einer sagt, er lebt nicht in Wien und hat nicht immer Zeit —

Der Gatte: Das ist doch nicht so unwahrscheinlich.

Das süsse Mädel: Ich glaub's nicht.

Der Gatte: Und da möchtest du dir gar kein Gewissen machen, daß du einen Ehemann zur Untreue verführst?

Das süsse Mädel: Ah was, deine Frau macht's sicher nicht anders als du.

Der Gatte: [sehr empört.] Du, das verbiet' ich mir. Solche Bemerkungen —

Das süsse Mädel: Du hast ja keine Frau, hab' ich geglaubt.

Der Gatte: Ob ich eine hab' oder nicht — man macht keine solche Bemerkungen. [Er ist aufgestanden.]

Das süsse Mädel: Karl, na Karl, was ist denn? Bist bös'? Schau, ich hab's ja wirklich nicht gewußt, daß du verheiratet

Husband: Well, how about ... coming here soon again ... or maybe somewhere else —

Sweet Young Girl: Don't know.

Husband: What do you mean, you don't know?

Sweet Young Girl: Well, you didn't have to ask, did you?

Husband: Alright then, when? I'd like to explain to you first of all that I don't live in Vienna. I only come here for a few days at a time, now and then.

Sweet Young Girl: Oh, go on, aren't you Viennese?

Husband: Certainly I'm Viennese. But I live out of town now.

Sweet Young Girl: Where?

Husband: Oh, what difference does it make.

Sweet Young Girl: Don't be afraid, I won't go there.

Husband: Oh, well, you could come if it would amuse you. I live in Graz.

Sweet Young Girl: You're married aren't you?

Husband: [Highly startled.] What makes you think that?

Sweet Young Girl: Oh, I just felt you were.

Husband: Wouldn't it upset you if I were?

Sweet Young Girl: Oh, I'd rather have you single, of course. But you are married?

Husband: I'd like to know what makes you think so?

Sweet Young Girl: When a man says he doesn't live in Vienna, and hasn't much time —

Husband: Well, that's not so improbable.

Sweet Young Girl: I don't believe it.

Husband: And your conscience wouldn't bother you at having led astray a married man?

Sweet Young Girl: Oh, go on, your wife's probably doing the same thing.

Husband: [Very indignant.] Now look here, I won't allow remarks like that!

Sweet Young Girl: I thought you didn't have a wife.

Husband: Whether I have or not is no excuse for saying things like that. [Stands up.]

Sweet Young Girl: Oh, now, Karl, what's the matter? Mad at me? Honest, I really didn't know you were married. I

bist. Ich hab' ja nur so g'redt. Geh' komm' und sei
wieder gut.

Der Gatte: [kommt nach ein paar Sekunden zu ihr.] Ihr seid
wirklich sonderbare Geschöpfe, ihr .... Weiber. [Er wird
wieder zärtlich an ihrer Seite.]

Das süsse Mädel: Geh' ..... nicht ..... es ist auch schon so spät. -

Der Gatte: Also jetzt hör' mir einmal zu. Reden wir einmal
im Ernst miteinander. Ich möcht' dich wieder sehen,
öfter wiedersehen.

Das süsse Mädel: Is wahr?

Der Gatte: Aber dazu ist notwendig .... also verlassen muß
ich mich auf dich können. Aufpassen kann ich nicht
auf dich.

Das süsse Mädel: Ah, ich pass' schon selber auf mich auf.

Der Gatte: Du bist .... na also, unerfahren kann man ja nicht
sagen — aber jung bist du — und — die Männer sind
im allgemeinen ein gewissenloses Volk.

Das süsse Mädel: Oh jeh!

Der Gatte: Ich mein' das nicht nur in moralischer Hinsicht.
— Na, du verstehst mich sicher. —

Das süsse Mädel: Ja, sag' mir, was glaubst du denn eigentlich
von mir?

Der Gatte: Also — wenn du mich lieb haben willst — nur
mich — so können wir's uns schon einrichten — wenn
ich auch für gewöhnlich in Graz wohne. Da wo jeden
Moment wer hereinkommen kann, ist es ja doch nicht
das rechte. [Das süsse Mädel schmiegt sich an ihn.] Das
nächste Mal ... werden wir wo anders zusammen sein,
ja?

Das süsse Mädel: Ja.

Der Gatte: Wo wir ganz ungestört sind.

Das süsse Mädel: Ja.

Der Gatte: [umfängt sie heiß.] Das andere besprechen wir im
Nachhausfahren. [Steht auf, öffnet die Thür.] Kellner
.... die Rechnung!

was just talking. Come on, please, be nice to me again.

Husband: [Goes to her after a few moments.] You certainly
are amazing creatures, you ... women. [Husband grows
tender again.]

Sweet Young Girl: No ... don't ... it's too late, anyway.

Husband: Then listen to me, will you? Let's talk seriously. I'd
like to see you again, often.

Sweet Young Girl: Would you, honest?

Husband: But in that case there must ... well, I've got to be
able to depend on you. I can't be watching you all the
time.

Sweet Young Girl: Oh, I can take care of myself.

Husband: You see, you're ... well, not exactly inexperienced
... but young — and — on the whole, men are an
unscrupulous race.

Sweet Young Girl: You don't say!

Husband: I don't mean that only in a moral sense — Well,
you understand me, surely —

Sweet Young Girl: Look here, what do you think I am,
anyway?

Husband: Well, then — if you really want to be my sweetheart
— mine alone — something can be arranged — even if I
do live in Graz most of the time. After all, a place where
people can walk in at any moment isn't the thing for
us. [Sweet young girl cuddles up to him.] Next time ...
we'll be together somewhere else, won't we?

Sweet Young Girl: Yes.

Husband: Where we can be entirely undisturbed.

Sweet Young Girl: Yes.

Husband: [Embracing her passionately.] We'll talk over the
details on the way home. [Stands up, opens the door.]
Waiter ... the check!

7: Das süsse Mädel und der Dichter

Ein kleines Zimmer, mit behaglichem Geschmack eingerichtet. Vorhänge, welche das Zimmer halbdunkel machen. Rote Stores. Großer Schreibtisch, auf dem Papiere und Bücher herumliegen. Ein Pianino an der Wand.

Das süße Mädel. Der Dichter. Sie kommen eben zusammen herein. Der Dichter schließt zu.

Der Dichter: So, mein Schatz [küßt sie.]

Das süsse Mädel: [mit Hut und Mantille.] Ah! Da ist aber schön! Nur sehen tut man nichts!

Der Dichter: Deine Augen müssen sich an das Halbdunkel gewöhnen. — Diese süßen Augen [küßt sie auf die Augen.]

Das süsse Mädel: Dazu werden die süßen Augen aber nicht Zeit genug haben.

Der Dichter: Warum denn?

Das süsse Mädel: Weil ich nur eine Minuten dableib'.

Der Dichter: Den Hut leg' ab, ja?

Das süsse Mädel: Wegen der einen Minuten?

Der Dichter: [nimmt die Nadel aus ihrem Hut und legt den Hut fort.] Und die Mantille —

Das süsse Mädel: Was willst denn? — Ich muß ja gleich wieder fortgehen.

Der Dichter: Aber du mußt dich doch ausruh'n! Wir sind ja drei Stunden gegangen.

Das süsse Mädel: Wir sind gefahren.

Der Dichter: Ja nach Haus — aber in Weidling am Bach sind wir doch drei volle Stunden herumgelaufen. Also setz' dich nur schön nieder, mein Kind .... wohin du willst; — hier an den Schreibtisch; — aber nein, das ist nicht

7: The Sweet Young Girl and the Poet

A small room, comfortably and tastefully furnished. Curtains that make the room half-dark. Red shades. Big desk, covered with papers and books. A small upright piano against the wall.

The sweet young girl and the poet enter together. The poet closes the door behind them.

Poet: There, my darling. [Kisses her.]

Sweet Young Girl: [Wearing a hat and coat.] Oh! How lovely it is here! Only one can't see a thing!

Poet: Your eyes'll have to get used to the semi-darkness. Those sweet eyes — [Kisses her eyes.]

Sweet Young Girl: These sweet eyes won't have time to do that, though.

Poet: Why not?

Sweet Young Girl: Because I'm only going to stay a minute.

Poet: But you'll take your hat off, won't you?

Sweet Young Girl: Just for a minute?

Poet: [Takes the pin from her hat and puts aside hat.] And the cloak —

Sweet Young Girl: What's the point? I have to go right away again.

Poet: But you must rest a little! We've been walking for three hours.

Sweet Young Girl: We've been driving.

Poet: Yes, on the way home — but we tramped around Weidling for three whole hours. So do sit down, my dear ... wherever you want; here at the desk; no, that's

bequem. Setz' dich auf den Divan. — So. [Er drückt sie nieder.] Bist du sehr müd', so kannst du dich auch hinlegen. So. [Er legt sie auf den Divan.] Da das Kopferl auf den Polster.

Das süsse Mädel: [lachend.] Aber ich bin ja gar nicht müd'!

Der Dichter: Das glaubst du nur. So — und wenn du schläfrig bist, kannst du auch schlafen. Ich werde ganz still sein. Übrigens kann ich dir ein Schlummerlied vorspielen ..... von mir .... [Geht zum Pianino.]

Das süsse Mädel: Von dir?

Der Dichter: Ja.

Das süsse Mädel: Ich hab' 'glaubt, Robert, du bist ein Doktor.

Der Dichter: Wieso? Ich hab' dir doch gesagt, daß ich Schriftsteller bin.

Das süsse Mädel: Die Schriftsteller sind doch alle Dokters.

Der Dichter: Nein; nicht alle. Ich z. B. nicht. Aber wie kommst du jetzt darauf.

Das süsse Mädel: Na, weil du sagst, das Stück, was du da spielen tust, ist von dir.

Der Dichter: Ja ... vielleicht ist es auch nicht von mir. Das ist ja ganz egal. Was? Überhaupt wer's gemacht hat, das ist immer egal. Nur schön muß es sein — nicht wahr?

Das süsse Mädel: Freilich .... schön muß es sein — das ist die Hauptsach'! —

Der Dichter: Weißt du, wie ich das gemeint hab'?

Das süsse Mädel: Was denn?

Der Dichter: Na, was ich eben gesagt hab'.

Das süsse Mädel: [schläfrig.] Na freilich.

Der Dichter: [steht auf; zu ihr, ihr das Haar streichelnd.] Kein Wort hast du verstanden.

Das süsse Mädel: Geh', ich bin doch nicht so dumm.

Der Dichter: Freilich bist du so dumm. Aber gerade darum hab' ich dich lieb. Ah, das ist so schön, wenn ihr dumm seid. Ich mein' in der Art wie du.

Das süsse Mädel: Geh', was schimpfst denn?

Der Dichter: Engel, kleiner. Nicht wahr, es liegt sich gut auf dem weichen, persischen Teppich?

not comfortable. Sit on the sofa. — There — [Pushes her down.] And if you're very tired you can lie down. There — [He stretches her out.] And now put your little head on the pillow.

Sweet Young Girl: [Laughing.] But I'm not in the least tired!

Poet: You think you're not. There — and if you get sleepy, just go ahead and sleep. I'll stay very quiet. I can play you a lullaby, too ... of my own ... [Goes to piano.]

Sweet Young Girl: Your own?

Poet: Yes.

Sweet Young Girl: I thought you were a doctor, Robert.

Poet: Why? I told you I was a writer.

Sweet Young Girl: But all the writers are doctors.

Poet: No; not all. I'm not, for instance. But what made you think of that now?

Sweet Young Girl: Well, because you said that the piece you're playing was your own.

Poet: Well — maybe it isn't mine. What difference does it make? Who cares who wrote it? It's enough that it's beautiful — isn't it?

Sweet Young Girl: Certainly. Just so it's beautiful — that's the chief thing.

Poet: Do you know what I meant?

Sweet Young Girl: Meant what?

Poet: What I just said.

Sweet Young Girl: [Sleepily.] Of course I did.

Poet: [Stands up, goes to her, strokes her hair.] You didn't understand a word.

Sweet Young Girl: Oh, go on, I'm not as stupid as all that.

Poet: Certainly you're that stupid. But that's just why I like you. Ah, it's so delightful when you women are stupid — the way you are, I mean.

Sweet Young Girl: Hey, stop being insulting!

Poet: Angel child! It feels good to lie on a soft Persian rug, doesn't it?

Das süsse Mädel: Oh ja. Geh', willst nicht weiter Klavier spielen?

Der Dichter: Nein, ich bin schon lieber da bei dir. [Streichelt sie.]

Das süsse Mädel: Geh', willst nicht lieber Licht machen?

Der Dichter: Oh nein .... Diese Dämmerung tut ja so wohl. Wir waren heute den ganzen Tag wie in Sonnenstrahlen gebadet. Jetzt sind wir sozusagen aus dem Bad gestiegen und schlagen .... die Dämmerung wie einen Badmantel [lacht.] ah nein — das muß anders gesagt werden .... Findest du nicht?

Das süsse Mädel: Weiß nicht.

Der Dichter: [sich leicht von ihr entfernend.] Göttlich, diese Dummheit! [Nimmt ein Notizbuch und schreibt ein paar Worte hinein.]

Das süsse Mädel: Was machst denn? [Sich nach ihm umwendend.] Was schreibst dir denn auf?

Der Dichter: [leise.] Sonne, Bad, Dämmerung, Mantel .... so .... [steckt das Notizbuch ein. Laut.]. Nichts .... Jetzt sag' einmal, mein Schatz, möchtest du nicht etwas essen oder trinken?

Das süsse Mädel: Durst hab' ich eigentlich keinen. Aber Appetit.

Der Dichter: Hm .... mir wär' lieber, du hättest Durst. Cognac hab' ich nämlich zu Haus, aber Essen müßte ich erst holen.

Das süsse Mädel: Kannst nichts holen lassen?

Der Dichter: Das ist schwer, meine Bedienerin ist jetzt nicht mehr da — na wart' — ich geh' schon selber .... was magst du denn?

Das süsse Mädel: Aber es zahlt sich ja wirklich nimmer aus, ich muß ja so wie so zu Haus.

Der Dichter: Kind, davon ist keine Rede. Aber ich werd' dir 'was sagen: wenn wir weggeh'n, geh'n wir zusammen wohin nachtmahlen.

Das süsse Mädel: Oh nein. Dazu hab' ich keine Zeit. Und dann, wohin sollen wir denn? Es könnt' uns ja 'wer Bekannter seh'n.

Sweet Young Girl: Oh, yes. Go on, play some more piano, won't you?

Poet: No, I'd rather stay here with you. [Strokes her.]

Sweet Young Girl: How about letting a little more light in?

Poet: Oh, no ... This twilight is soothing. We've been practically bathed in sunlight the whole day. Now, having emerged from our bath we're throwing the mantle of twilight over ourselves ... [Laughs.] ... Ah, no — that should be said another way ... Don't you think so?

Sweet Young Girl: Don't know.

Poet: [Drawing away from her slightly.] Divine stupidity! [Takes out a notebook and scribbles a few words in it.]

Sweet Young Girl: What are you doing? [Turning towards him.] What are you writing?

Poet: Sun, bath, twilight, cloak ... there ... [Puts back the notebook. Then, aloud.] Nothing ... Now tell me, my sweet, wouldn't you like something to eat or drink?

Sweet Young Girl: I'm not at all thirsty, but I am hungry.

Poet: Hmmm ... I'd rather you were thirsty. I have some Cognac in the house, but I'd have to go out to get food.

Sweet Young Girl: Can't someone get it for you?

Poet: That's difficult, my servant isn't here just now — but wait — I'll go myself. What would you like?

Sweet Young Girl: But it's really hardly worthwhile, I have to go home, anyway.

Poet: Child, there's no thought of that. But I'll tell you something; when we leave here we'll go somewhere for supper.

Sweet Young Girl: Oh, no. I haven't time for that. Where would we go anyway. Some friend might see us.

Der Dichter: Hast du denn gar so viel Bekannte?

Das süsse Mädel: Es braucht uns ja nur Einer zu seh'n, ist's Malheur schon fertig.

Der Dichter: Was ist denn das für ein Malheur?

Das süsse Mädel: Na, was glaubst, wenn die Mutter 'was hört ....

Der Dichter: Wir können ja doch irgend wohin gehen, wo uns niemand sieht, es gibt ja Gasthäuser mit einzelnen Zimmern.

Das süsse Mädel: [singend.] Ja, beim Souper im chambre separée!

Der Dichter: Warst du schon einmal in einem chambre separée?

Das süsse Mädel: Wenn ich die Wahrheit sagen soll — ja.

Der Dichter: Wer war der Glückliche?

Das süsse Mädel: Oh das ist nicht, wie du meinst .... ich war mit meiner Freundin und ihrem Bräutigam. Die haben mich mitgenommen.

Der Dichter: So. Und das soll ich dir am End' glauben?

Das süsse Mädel: Brauchst mir ja nicht zu glauben!

Der Dichter: [nah bei ihr.] Bist du jetzt rot geworden? Man sieht nichts mehr! Ich kann deine Züge nicht mehr ausnehmen. [Mit seiner Hand berührt er ihre Wangen.] Aber auch so erkenn' ich dich.

Das süsse Mädel: Na, pass' nur auf, daß du mich mit keiner andern verwechselst.

Der Dichter: Es ist seltsam, ich kann mich nicht mehr erinnern, wie du aussiehst.

Das süsse Mädel: Dank' schön!

Der Dichter: [ernst.] Du, das ist beinah' unheimlich, ich kann mir dich nicht vorstellen — In einem gewissen Sinne hab' ich dich schon vergessen — Wenn ich mich auch nicht mehr an den Klang deiner Stimme erinnern könnte .... was wärst du da eigentlich? — Nah und fern zugleich .... unheimlich.

Das süsse Mädel: Geh', was redst denn —?

Der Dichter: Nichts, mein Engel, nichts. Wo sind deine Lippen .... [Er küßt sie.]

Poet: Have you so many friends?
Sweet Young Girl: Well, one is enough to get us into trouble.

Poet: What kind of trouble?
Sweet Young Girl: Well, suppose my mother heard about it ...

Poet: But we can go somewhere where no one'll see us, there are restaurants with private rooms.

Sweet Young Girl: [Chanting.] Yes, supper in a private room!

Poet: Have you ever been in a private room?

Sweet Young Girl: To tell the truth — yes.
Poet: Who was the lucky fellow?
Sweet Young Girl: Oh, not the way you think ... I was with a girl friend and her fiancé. They took me along.

Poet: I see. I'm supposed to believe that!
Sweet Young Girl: You don't have to believe it!
Poet: [Close to her.] Did you blush just now? One can't see a thing, it's so dark. I can't even distinguish your features. [Touches her cheek with his hand.] But I can identify you this way just as well.
Sweet Young Girl: Well, see that you don't mistake me for somebody else.
Poet: It's strange, I can't remember anymore what you look like.
Sweet Young Girl: Thank you kindly!
Poet: [Serious.] No, really, it's uncanny, I simply can't visualize you. In a certain sense I've forgotten you already. — If I were to forget the sound of your voice too ... what would you be then? — Near and far at the same time ... uncanny.

Sweet Young Girl: What are you raving about?
Poet: Nothing, angel, nothing. Where are your lips? ... [Kisses her.]

Das süsse Mädel: Willst nicht lieber Licht machen?

Der Dichter: Nein .... [Er wird sehr zärtlich.] Sag', ob du mich lieb hast.

Das süsse Mädel: Sehr .... oh sehr!

Der Dichter: Hast du schon irgendwen so lieb gehabt wie mich?

Das süsse Mädel: Ich hab' dir ja schon gesagt nein.

Der Dichter: Aber .... [er seufzt.]

Das süsse Mädel: Das ist ja mein Bräutigam gewesen.

Der Dichter: Es wär' mir lieber, du würdest jetzt nicht an ihn denken.

Das süsse Mädel: Geh' ... was machst denn ... schau ...

Der Dichter: Wir können uns jetzt auch vorstellen, daß wir in einem Schloß in Indien sind.

Das süsse Mädel: Dort sind s' gewiß nicht so schlimm wie du.

Der Dichter: Wie blöd! Göttlich — Ah wenn du ahntest, was du für mich bist ....

Das süsse Mädel: Na?

Der Dichter: Stoß' mich doch nicht immer weg; ich tu' dir ja nichts — vorläufig.

Das süsse Mädel: Du, das Mieder tut mir weh.

Der Dichter: [einfach.] Zieh's aus.

Das süsse Mädel: Ja. Aber du darfst deswegen nicht schlimm werden.

Der Dichter: Nein. [Das süsse Mädel hat sich erhoben und zieht in der Dunkelheit ihr Mieder aus. Der Dichter: der währenddessen auf dem Divan sitzt.] Sag', interessiert's dich's denn gar nicht, wie ich mit dem Zunamen heiß'?

Das süsse Mädel: Ja, wie heißt du denn?

Der Dichter: Ich werd' dir lieber nicht sagen, wie ich heiß', sondern wie ich mich nenne.

Das süsse Mädel: Was ist denn da für ein Unterschied?

Der Dichter: Na, wie ich mich als Schriftsteller nenne.

Das süsse Mädel: Ah, du schreibst nicht unter deinem wirklichen Namen? [Der Dichter nah zu ihr.] Ah .... geh!.... nicht.

Der Dichter: Was einem da für ein Duft entgegensteigt. Wie süß. [Er küßt ihren Busen.]

Sweet Young Girl: Hadn't you better turn on the lights?
Poet: No. [Growing very affectionate.] Tell me, do you love me?
Sweet Young Girl: Oh, a lot ... a lot!
Poet: Have you ever loved anyone as much as me?

Sweet Young Girl: I've already told you, no.
Poet: But ... [Sighs.]
Sweet Young Girl: He was my fiancé.
Poet: I wish you wouldn't think about him now.

Sweet Young Girl: Say ... what are you doing ... see here ...
Poet: Let's imagine now that we're in some place in Inda.

Sweet Young Girl: They wouldn't be as wicked as you, there.

Poet: How idiotic! Divine — ah, if you only realized what you mean to me ...
Sweet Young Girl: Well?
Poet: Stop pushing me away all the time; I'm not doing anything to you — yet.
Sweet Young Girl: My corset hurts me.
Poet: [Simply.] Take it off.
Sweet Young Girl: Yes. But you mustn't be naughty because I do.
Poet: No. [Sweet young girl stands up, takes off corset in darkness. Poet remains on the sofa.] By the way, haven't you any desire at all to know my name?

Sweet Young Girl: Yes, what is it?
Poet: I'd rather not tell you my name. I'll tell you what I call myself, instead.
Sweet Young Girl: What's the difference?
Poet: Well, what I call myself professionally — as a writer.
Sweet Young Girl: Oh, you don't write under your real name? [Poet comes close to her.] Now don't! ... go away!

Poet: What fragrance emanates from your body. How sweet ... [Kisses her breast.]

Das süsse Mädel: Du zerreißt ja mein Hemd.

Der Dichter: Weg .... weg .... alles das ist überflüssig.

Das süsse Mädel: Aber Robert!

Der Dichter: Und jetzt komm' in unser indisches Schloß.

Das süsse Mädel: Sag' mir zuerst, ob du mich wirklich lieb hast.

Der Dichter: Aber ich bete dich ja an. [Küßt sie heiß.] Ich bete dich ja an, mein Schatz, mein Frühling ... mein ...

Das süsse Mädel: Robert .... Robert ....

* * * * *

Der Dichter: Das war überirdische Seligkeit .... Ich nenne mich ....

Das süsse Mädel: Robert, oh mein Robert!

Der Dichter: Ich nenne mich Biebitz.

Das süsse Mädel: Warum nennst du dich Biebitz?

Der Dichter: Ich heiße nicht Biebitz — ich nenne mich so .... nun, kennst du den Namen vielleicht nicht?

Das süsse Mädel: Nein.

Der Dichter: Du kennst den Namen Biebitz nicht? Ah — göttlich! Wirklich? Du sagst es nur, daß du ihn nicht kennst, nicht wahr?

Das süsse Mädel: Meiner Seel', ich hab' ihn nie gehört!

Der Dichter: Gehst du denn nie ins Theater?

Das süsse Mädel: Oh ja — ich war erst neulich mit einem — weißt, mit dem Onkel von meiner Freundin und meiner Freundin sind wir in der Oper gewesen bei der Cavalleria.

Der Dichter: Hm, also ins Burgtheater gehst du nie.

Das süsse Mädel: Da krieg ich nie Karten geschenkt.

Der Dichter: Ich werde dir nächstens eine Karte schicken.

Das süsse Mädel: Oh ja! aber nicht vergessen! Zu 'was Lustigem aber.

Der Dichter: Ja ..... lustig ..... zu 'was Traurigem willst du nicht geh'n?

Das süsse Mädel: Nicht gern.

Der Dichter: Auch wenn's ein Stück von mir ist?

Das süsse Mädel: Geh' — ein Stück von dir? Du schreibst für's Theater?

Sweet Young Girl: You're tearing my chemise.

Poet: Away ... away with all these inessentials.

Sweet Young Girl: But, Robert ... !

Poet: And now let's go to our Indian palace.

Sweet Young Girl: First tell me that you really love me.

Poet: But I adore you — [Kisses her passionately.] — I worship you, my treasure, my springtime ... my ...

Sweet Young Girl: Robert ... Robert ... !

* * * * *

Poet: That was transcendental bliss ... I'm called ...

Sweet Young Girl: Robert, my Robert!

Poet: I'm called Biebitz.

Sweet Young Girl: Why are you called Biebitz?

Poet: Biebitz isn't my name — I'm just called Biebitz ... Well, don't you know the name?

Sweet Young Girl: No.

Poet: You haven't heard the name Biebitz? Ah — divine! Really? You're only pretending you don't know it, aren't you?

Sweet Young Girl: Honest to God, I've never heard of it!

Poet: Don't you ever go to the theatre?

Sweet Young Girl: Oh, yes — I went just the other night — with my girl friend and her uncle — we went to the opera to hear Cavalleria.

Poet: Hmmm, so you never go to the Royal Theatre?

Sweet Young Girl: Nobody ever sends me tickets for that.

Poet: I'll send you a ticket.

Sweet Young Girl: Oh, lovely! But don't forget! And send one for something funny.

Poet: Oh ... funny ... you don't want to see something sad?

Sweet Young Girl: Not very much.

Poet: Even if it's a play I wrote?

Sweet Young Girl: A play you wrote? You write for the theatre?

Der Dichter: Erlaube, ich will nur Licht machen. Ich habe dich noch nicht gesehen, seit du meine Geliebte bist. — Engel! [Er zündet eine Kerze an.]

Das süsse Mädel: Geh', ich schäm' mich ja. Gib mir wenigstens eine Decke.

Der Dichter: Später! [Er kommt mit dem Licht zu ihr, betrachtet sie lang.]

Das süsse Mädel: [bedeckt ihr Gesicht mit den Händen.] Geh', Robert!

Der Dichter: Du bist schön, du bist die Schönheit, du bist vielleicht sogar die Natur, du bist die heilige Einfalt.

Das süsse Mädel: Oh weh, du tropfst mich ja an! Schau, was gibst denn nicht acht!

Der Dichter: [stellt die Kerze weg.] Du bist das, was ich seit lange gesucht habe. Du liebst nur mich, du würdest mich auch lieben, wenn ich Schnittwarencommis wäre. Das tut wohl. Ich will dir gestehen, daß ich einen gewissen Verdacht bis zu diesem Moment nicht losgeworden bin. Sag' ehrlich, hast du nicht geahnt, daß ich Biebitz bin?

Das süsse Mädel: Aber geh', ich weiß gar nicht, was du von mir willst. Ich kenn' ja gar kein' Biebitz.

Der Dichter: Was ist der Ruhm! Nein, vergiß, was ich gesagt habe, vergiß sogar den Namen, den ich dir gesagt hab'. Robert bin ich und will ich für dich bleiben. Ich hab' auch nur gescherzt. [Leicht.] Ich bin ja nicht Schriftsteller, ich bin Commis und am Abend spiel' ich bei Volkssängern Klavier.

Das süsse Mädel: Ja, jetzt kenn' ich mich aber nicht mehr aus ...... nein, und wie du einen nur anschaust. Ja, was ist denn, ja was hast denn?

Der Dichter: Es ist sehr sonderbar — was mir beinah' noch nie passiert ist, mein Schatz, mir sind die Tränen nah. Du ergreifst mich tief. Wir wollen zusammen bleiben, ja? Wir werden einander sehr lieb haben.

Das süsse Mädel: Du, ist das wahr mit den Volkssängern?

Der Dichter: Ja, aber frag' nicht weiter. Wenn du mich lieb hast, frag' überhaupt nichts. Sag', kannst du dich auf

Poet: Excuse me, but I want to light up. I haven't seen you since you've been my sweetheart. Angel! [Lights a candle.]

Sweet Young Girl: Oh, lord, I feel so ashamed. At least give me a cover.

Poet: Later! [Approaches her with the candle, surveys her at length.]

Sweet Young Girl: [Covering her face with her hands.] Now don't, Robert!

Poet: You are beautiful, you are beauty itself, you are Nature, you are holy simplicity.

Sweet Young Girl: Ouch, you're dripping that candle on me! Look out, can't you?

Poet: [Putting aside the candle.] You are what I've been searching for a long time. You love me, and me alone — you'd love me if I were only a dry-goods clerk. That's a wonderful feeling. I confess that I've been harboring a certain doubt up to this moment. Tell me honestly, didn't you suspect that I was Biebitz?

Sweet Young Girl: Oh, heavens, what are you driving at, anyway? I don't know any Biebitz.

Poet: Such is fame! No, forget what I told you, forget the name I told you too. I'm Robert to you and always will be. I was only joking. [Lightly.] I'm not a playwright at all, I'm a salesman, and I play the piano for choral societies at night.

Sweet Young Girl: Now I can't make you out at all ... and my goodness, the way you stare at me. What's the matter, anyway, what's wrong?

Poet: It's so extraordinary — something that's hardly ever happened to me before, my sweet — the tears are coming to my eyes. You move me deeply. We'll stay together, won't we? We'll love each other very much.

Sweet Young Girl: Say, is that true about the choral societies?

Poet: Yes, but don't ask anymore. If you love me, stop asking questions. Tell me, can you manage to make yourself

ein paar Wochen ganz frei machen?

Das süsse Mädel: Wieso ganz frei?

Der Dichter: Nun, vom Hause weg?

Das süsse Mädel: Aber!! Wie kann ich das! Was möcht' die Mutter sagen? Und dann, ohne mich ging' ja alles schief zu Haus.

Der Dichter: Ich hatte es mir schön vorgestellt, mit dir zusammen, allein mit dir, irgendwo in der Einsamkeit draußen, im Wald, in der Natur ein paar Wochen zu leben. Natur .... in der Natur. Und dann, eines Tages Adieu — von einander gehen, ohne zu wissen, wohin.

Das süsse Mädel: Jetzt redst schon vom Adieusagen! Und ich hab' gemeint, daß du mich so gern hast.

Der Dichter: Gerade darum — [Beugt sich zu ihr und küßt sie auf die Stirn.] Du süßes Geschöpf!

Das süsse Mädel: Geh', halt mich fest, mir ist so kalt.

Der Dichter: Es wird Zeit sein, daß du dich ankleidest. Warte, ich zünde dir noch ein paar Kerzen an.

Das süsse Mädel: [erhebt sich.] Nicht herschauen.

Der Dichter: Nein. [Am Fenster.] Sag' mir, mein Kind, bist du glücklich?

Das süsse Mädel: Wie meinst das?

Der Dichter: Ich mein' im allgemeinen, ob du glücklich bist?

Das süsse Mädel: Es könnt' schon besser gehen.

Der Dichter: Du mißverstehst mich. Von deinen häuslichen Verhältnissen hast du mir ja schon genug erzählt. Ich weiß, daß du keine Prinzessin bist. Ich mein', wenn du von alledem absiehst, wenn du dich einfach leben spürst. Spürst du dich überhaupt leben?

Das süsse Mädel: Geh', hast kein' Kamm?

Der Dichter: [geht zum Toilettetisch, gibt ihr den Kamm, betrachtet das süße Mädel.] Herrgott, siehst du so entzückend aus!

Das süsse Mädel: Na .... nicht!

Der Dichter: Geh', bleib' noch da, bleib' da, ich hol' 'was zum Nachtmahl und ....

Das süsse Mädel: Aber es ist ja schon viel zu spät.

Der Dichter: Es ist noch nicht neun.

free for a few weeks?

Sweet Young Girl: What do you mean, free?

Poet: Well, away from home.

Sweet Young Girl: What an idea! How could I do that? What would mother say? And then, if I weren't there everything would go wrong at home.

Poet: I'd imagined it all so beautifully, we two together, going off somewhere in the great solitude, into the forest, into Nature, to live for a few weeks. Nature ... into Nature. And then, one day, Adieu — to part from each other, without knowing where we will go.

Sweet Young Girl: Now you're talking of saying goodbye already! And I thought you liked me so much.

Poet: That's just why — [Bends over her and kisses her brow.] You adorable creature!

Sweet Young Girl: Come, hold me tight, I'm so cold.

Poet: I suppose it's time for you to get dressed. Wait, I'll light a few more candles.

Sweet Young Girl: Don't look.

Poet: No. [At the window.] Tell me, my child, are you happy?

Sweet Young Girl: How do you mean?

Poet: I mean, do you lead a happy life?

Sweet Young Girl: It could be better.

Poet: You misunderstand me. You've told me enough about your domestic circumstances. I know that you're no princess. I mean, putting material things aside — just feeling yourself alive. As a matter of fact, do you feel yourself actually living?

Sweet Young Girl: Say, haven't you any comb?

Poet: [Goes to dressing-table, gives her comb, gazes at her.] God in heaven, how enchanting you look!

Sweet Young Girl: Now ... don't!

Poet: Please, stay a while longer, stay here, I'll get something for supper and ...

Sweet Young Girl: But it's much too late now.

Poet: It isn't nine yet.

Das süsse Mädel: Na, sei so gut, da muß ich mich aber tummeln.

Der Dichter: Wann werden wir uns denn wiedersehen?

Das süsse Mädel: Na, wann willst mich denn wiedersehen?

Der Dichter: Morgen.

Das süsse Mädel: Was ist denn morgen für ein Tag?

Der Dichter: Samstag.

Das süsse Mädel: Oh da kann ich nicht, da muß ich mit meiner kleinen Schwester zum Vormund.

Der Dichter: Also Sonntag .... hm .... Sonntag .... am Sonntag .... jetzt werd' ich dir 'was erklären. — Ich bin nicht Biebitz, aber Biebitz ist mein Freund. Ich werd' dir ihn einmal vorstellen. Aber Sonntag ist das Stück von Biebitz; ich werd' dir eine Karte schicken und werde dich dann vom Theater abholen. Du wirst mir sagen, wie dir das Stück gefallen hat; ja?

Das süsse Mädel: Jetzt, die G'schicht' mit dem Biebitz — da bin ich schon ganz blöd.

Der Dichter: Völlig werd' ich dich erst kennen, wenn ich weiß, was du bei diesem Stück empfunden hast.

Das süsse Mädel: So ..., ich bin fertig.

Der Dichter: Komm', mein Schatz! [Sie gehen.]

Sweet Young Girl: No, please, I've got to run along.

Poet: When will we see each other again?
Sweet Young Girl: Well, when do you want to see me?
Poet: Tomorrow.
Sweet Young Girl: What day is tomorrow?
Poet: Saturday.
Sweet Young Girl: Oh, I can't then. I have to take my little sister to her godfather.
Poet: Alright then, Sunday ... hmmm ... on Sunday ... let me explain something to you — I'm not Biebitz, but Biebitz is a friend of mine. I'll introduce him to you sometime. Well, on Sunday Biebitz's play is being given. I'll send you a ticket and then I'll pick you up at the theatre afterwards. You'll tell me how you liked the play, won't you?
Sweet Young Girl: Honest, this Biebitz business — I'm all mixed up now.
Poet: I won't really know you until I've found out how you reacted towards this play.
Sweet Young Girl: There ... I'm ready now.
Poet: Let's go, my love! [They leave.]

8: Der Dichter und die Schauspielerin

Ein Zimmer in einem Gasthof auf dem Land. Es ist ein
Frühlingsabend; über den Wiesen und Hügeln liegt der
Mond; die Fenster stehen offen. Große Stille.

Der Dichter und die Schauspielerin treten ein; wie sie
hereintreten, verlöscht das Licht, das der Dichter in der
Hand hält.

Dichter: Oh ....

Schauspielerin: Was ist denn?

Dichter: Das Licht. — Aber wir brauchen keins. Schau', es
ist ganz hell. Wunderbar! [Schauspielerin sinkt am
Fenster plötzlich nieder, mit gefalteten Händen.] Was
hast du denn? [Schauspielerin schweigt.] Was machst
du denn?

Schauspielerin: [empört.] Siehst du nicht, daß ich bete? —

Dichter: Glaubst du an Gott?

Schauspielerin: Gewiß, ich bin ja kein blasser Schurke.

Dichter: Ach so!

Schauspielerin: Komm' doch zu mir, knie dich neben mich
hin. Kannst wirklich auch einmal beten. Wird dir keine
Perle aus der Krone fallen. [Dichter kniet neben sie hin
und umfaßt sie.] Wüstling! — [Erhebt sich.] Und weißt
du auch, zu wem ich gebetet habe?

Dichter: Zu Gott, nehm' ich an.

Schauspielerin: [Großer Hohn.] Jawohl! zu dir hab' ich
gebetet.

Dichter: Warum hast du denn da zum Fenster hin-
ausgeschaut?

Schauspielerin: Sag' mir lieber, wo du mich da hingeschleppt
hast, Verführer!

8: The Poet and the Actress

Room in a country Inn. A Spring night. The moon shines over the hills and fields. The windows are open. Deep silence.

The poet and the Actress enter. As they do so, the lighted candle in the poet's hand goes out.

Poet: Oh ...

Actress: What's the matter?

Poet: The light. — But we don't need any. Look, it's quite bright. Marvelous! [Actress suddenly sinks down on her knees before window, with folded hands.] What's the matter? [No answer.] What are you doing?

Actress: [Indignant.] Can't you see I'm praying?

Poet: Do you believe in God?

Actress: Of course, I'm no bloody heathen.

Poet: I see.

Actress: Come along, kneel next to me. You might pray for once, too. It won't put a dent in your halo. [Poet kneels next to her and embraces her.] Libertine! [Gets up.] Do you happen to know whom I was praying to?

Poet: To God, I suppose.

Actress: [With great irony.] Yes! I was praying to you.

Poet: Then why did you look out of the window?

Actress: I'd rather you told me where you've dragged me to — you seducer!

Dichter: Aber Kind, das war ja deine Idee. Du wolltest ja auf's Land — und gerade hieher.

Schauspielerin: Nun, hab' ich nicht recht gehabt?

Dichter: Gewiß; es ist ja entzückend hier. Wenn man bedenkt, zwei Stunden von Wien — und die völlige Einsamkeit. Und was für eine Gegend!

Schauspielerin: Was? Da könntest du wohl mancherlei dichten, wenn du zufällig Talent hättest.

Dichter: Warst du hier schon einmal?

Schauspielerin: Ob ich hier schon war? Ha! Hier hab' ich jahrelang gelebt!

Dichter: Mit wem?

Schauspielerin: Nun, mit Fritz natürlich.

Dichter: Ach so!

Schauspielerin: Den Mann hab' ich wohl angebetet! —

Dichter: Das hast du mir bereits erzählt.

Schauspielerin: Ich bitte — ich kann auch wieder gehen, wenn ich dich langweile!

Dichter: Du mich langweilen?.... Du ahnst ja gar nicht, was du für mich bedeutest .... Du bist eine Welt für sich .... Du bist das Göttliche, du bist das Genie .... Du bist .... Du bist eigentlich die heilige Einfalt .... Ja, Du .... Aber du solltest jetzt nicht von Fritz reden.

Schauspielerin: Das war wohl eine Verirrung! Na! —

Dichter: Es ist schön, daß du das einsiehst.

Schauspielerin: Komm, her, gib mir einen Kuß! [Dichter küßt sie.] Jetzt wollen wir uns aber eine gute Nacht sagen! Leb' wohl, mein Schatz!

Dichter: Wie meinst du das?

Schauspielerin: Nun, ich werde mich schlafen legen!

Dichter: Ja, — das schon, aber was das gute Nacht sagen anbelangt .... Wo soll denn ich übernachten?

Schauspielerin: Es gibt gewiß noch viele Zimmer in diesem Haus.

Dichter: Die anderen haben aber keinen Reiz für mich. Jetzt werd' ich übrigens Licht machen, meinst du nicht?

Schauspielerin: Ja.

Dichter: [zündet das Licht an, das auf dem Nachtkästchen

Poet: But, my dear child, this was your idea. You wanted to go to the country — and this place especially.

Actress: Well, wasn't it a good idea?

Poet: Certainly; it's enchanting here. When you consider that it's only two hours from Vienna — and then this utter solitude. And what lovely country!

Actress: Gorgeous, isn't it? You could write a great deal here if you had any talent.

Poet: Have you been here before?

Actress: Have I been here before? Ha! I've lived here for years!

Poet: With whom?

Actress: With Fritz, of course.

Poet: I see.

Actress: How I adored that man!

Poet: So you've told me.

Actress: A thousand pardons — I can just as well go if I bore you!

Poet: You bore me? ... You haven't the faintest idea what you mean to me ... You're a whole world in itself ... You are divine, you are genius itself ... You are ... you are godly simplicity ... Truly, you ... But you shouldn't talk about Fritz now.

Actress: There must have been an aberration. There!

Poet: It's fine of you to admit that.

Actress: Come here, give me a kiss! [Poet kisses her.] Now let's say goodnight! Farewell, my pet!

Poet: What do you mean, "farewell"?

Actress: Well, I'm going to bed.

Poet: That's alright, but as for this "good night" business ... where am I supposed to spend the night?

Actress: There are surely many other rooms in this house.

Poet: Other rooms don't attract me. Anyway, I'd better light up here, hadn't I?

Actress: Yes.

Poet: [Lights a candle on the night-table.] What a pretty

steht.] Was für ein hübsches Zimmer .... und fromm
sind die Leute hier. Lauter Heiligenbilder .... Es
wäre interessant, eine Zeit unter diesen Menschen
zu verbringen .... doch eine andre Welt. Wir wissen
eigentlich so wenig von den andern.

Schauspielerin: Rede keinen Stiefel und reiche mir lieber
diese Tasche vom Tisch herüber.

Dichter: Hier, meine Einzige! [Schauspielerin nimmt aus
dem Täschchen ein kleines, gerahmtes Bildchen, stellt
es auf das Nachtkästchen.] Was ist das?

Schauspielerin: Das ist die Madonna.

Dichter: Die hast du immer mit?

Schauspielerin: Die ist doch mein Talisman. Und jetzt geh',
Robert!

Dichter: Aber was sind das für Scherze? Soll ich dir nicht
helfen?

Schauspielerin: Nein, du sollst jetzt geh'n.

Dichter: Und wann soll ich wiederkommen?

Schauspielerin: In zehn Minuten.

Dichter: [küßt sie.] Auf Wiedersehen!

Schauspielerin: Wo willst du denn hin?

Dichter: Ich werde vor dem Fenster auf und abgehen. Ich
liebe es sehr, nachts im Freien herumzuspazieren.
Meine besten Gedanken kommen mir so. Und gar
in deiner Nähe, von deiner Sehnsucht sozusagen
umhaucht .... in deiner Kunst webend.

Schauspielerin: Du redest wie ein Idiot ....

Dichter: [schmerzlich.] Es gibt Frauen, welche vielleicht
sagen würden .... wie ein Dichter.

Schauspielerin: Nun geh' endlich. Aber fang' mir kein
Verhältnis mit der Kellnerin an. [Dichter geht.
Schauspielerin kleidet sich aus. Sie hört, wie der
Dichter über die Holztreppe hinuntergeht und hört
jetzt seine Schritte unter dem Fenster. Sie geht, sobald
sie ausgekleidet ist, zum Fenster, sieht hinunter, er
steht da; sie ruft flüsternd hinunter.] Komm'! [Dichter
kommt rasch herauf; stürzt zu ihr, die sich unterdessen

room ... the people here are very pious ... lots of holy pictures ... it would be interesting to spend some time among these natives ... it's another world altogether. We know so little about other people, actually.

Actress: Stop talking rot and hand me my purse from the table.

Poet: Here, my only beloved! [Actress takes a little framed picture from her purse and puts it on the night-table.] What's that?

Actress: That's the Madonna.

Poet: You always carry her with you?

Actress: Certainly, she's my talisman. Now go, Robert!

Poet: You're joking. Can't I help you?

Actress: No, you can go.

Poet: When shall I come back?

Actress: In ten minutes.

Poet: [Kisses her.] So long, then!

Actress: Where will you go?

Poet: I'll walk up and down in front of the window. I'm very fond of walking about outdoors at night. My best ideas come to me that way. And especially near you, enveloped — so to speak — in my longing for you ... enmeshed in your art.

Actress: You talk like an idiot.

Poet: [Hurt.] Some women would have said ... like a poet.

Actress: Now hurry up and go. But don't start any flirtation with the chambermaid. [Poet goes. Actress undresses. She hears the poet clattering down the wooden stairs, and later hears his footsteps outside the window. As soon as she is undressed, she goes to the windwo, looks down below where he is standing, and whispers to him.] Come! [Poet rushes upstairs and into the room, just as she has slipped into bed and blown out

ins Bett gelegt und das Licht ausgelöscht hat; er sperrt
ab.] So, jetzt kannst du dich zu mir setzen und mir 'was
erzählen.

Dichter: [setzt sich zu ihr auf's Bett.] Soll ich nicht das Fenster
schließen? Ist dir nicht kalt?

Schauspielerin: Oh nein!

Dichter: Was soll ich dir denn erzählen?

Schauspielerin: Nun, wem bist du in diesem Moment untreu?

Dichter: Ich bin es ja leider noch nicht.

Schauspielerin: Nun, tröste dich, ich betrüge auch jemanden.

Dichter: Das kann ich mir denken.

Schauspielerin: Und was glaubst du, wen?

Dichter: Ja Kind, davon kann ich keine Ahnung haben.

Schauspielerin: Nun, rate.

Dichter: Warte .... Na, deinen Direktor.

Schauspielerin: Mein Lieber, ich bin keine Choristin.

Dichter: Nun, ich dachte nur.

Schauspielerin: Rate noch einmal.

Dichter: Also du betrügst deinen Kollegen ... Benno —

Schauspielerin: Ha! Der Mann liebt ja überhaupt keine Frauen
.... weißt du das nicht? Der Mann hat ja ein Verhältnis
mit seinem Briefträger!

Dichter: Ist das möglich! —

Schauspielerin: So gib mir lieber einen Kuß! [Dichter
umschlingt sie.] Aber was tust du denn?

Dichter: So quäl' mich doch nicht so.

Schauspielerin: Höre, Robert, ich werde dir einen Vorschlag
machen. Leg' dich zu mir ins Bett.

Dichter: Angenommen!

Schauspielerin: Komm' schnell, komm' schnell!

Dichter: Ja .... wenn es nach mir gegangen wäre, wär' ich
schon längst .... Hörst du ....

Schauspielerin: Was denn?

Dichter: Draußen zirpen die Grillen.

Schauspielerin: Du bist wohl wahnsinnig, mein Kind, hier
gibt es ja keine Grillen.

Dichter: Aber du hörst sie doch.

Schauspielerin: Nun' so komm, endlich!

the candle, and locks the door.] There, now you can sit down next to me and tell me things.

Poet: [sits near her on the bed] Don't you want me to shut the window? Aren't you cold?

Actress: Oh, no.

Poet: What do you want me to tell you?

Actress: Well, whom are you unfaithful to at this moment?

Poet: Unfortunately to no one, just yet.

Actress: Well, console yourself, I'm deceiving somebody too.

Poet: I don't doubt that.

Actress: And who do you think it is?

Poet: My dear, how can I possibly know.

Actress: Well, guess.

Poet: Wait ... your director.

Actress: Darling, I'm not a chorus-girl.

Poet: Well, I just thought ...

Actress: Guess again.

Poet: You're deceiving your leading man ... Benno —

Actress: Ha! He doesn't love any woman ... didn't you know that? He's having an affair with the postman!

Poet: You don't say!

Actress: Come, give me a kiss. [Poet throws his arms about her.] What do you think you're doing?

Poet: Well, don't torture me so.

Actress: Listen, Robert, I have a suggestion. Lie down next to me.

Poet: Sold!

Actress: Hurry, hurry!

Poet: See here, if I'd have had my way, I'd have been there long ago ... Listen.

Actress: What?

Poet: The crickets are chirping outside.

Actress: You're crazy, my pet, there aren't any crickets hereabouts.

Poet: But you hear them, don't you?

Actress: Oh, hurry up and come!

Dichter: Da bin ich. [Zu ihr.]

Schauspielerin: So, jetzt bleib' schön ruhig liegen ..... Pst ..... nicht rühren.

Dichter: Ja, was fällt dir denn ein?

Schauspielerin: Du möchtest wohl gerne ein Verhältnis mit mir haben?

Dichter: Das dürfte dir doch bereits klar sein.

Schauspielerin: Nun, das möchte wohl mancher ....

Dichter: Es ist aber doch nicht zu bezweifeln, daß in diesem Moment ich die meisten Chancen habe.

Schauspielerin: So komm', meine Grille! Ich werde dich von nun an Grille nennen.

Dichter: Schön ....

Schauspielerin: Nun, wen betrüg' ich?

Dichter: Wen?.... Vielleicht mich ....

Schauspielerin: Mein Kind, du bist schwer gehirnleidend.

Dichter: Oder einen ..... den du selbst nie gesehen ..... einen, den du nicht kennst, einen − der für dich bestimmt ist und den du nie finden kannst ....

Schauspielerin: Ich bitte dich, rede nicht so märchenhaft blöd.

Dichter: .... Ist es nicht sonderbar, ... auch du − und man sollte doch glauben − Aber nein, es hieße dir dein bestes rauben, wollte man dir .... komm', komm' − komm' −

* * * * *

Schauspielerin: Das ist doch schöner, als in blödsinnigen Stücken spielen .... was meinst du?

Dichter: Nun, ich mein', es ist gut, daß du doch zuweilen in vernünftigen zu spielen hast.

Schauspielerin: Du arroganter Hund meinst gewiß wieder das deine?

Dichter: Jawohl!

Schauspielerin: [ernst.] Das ist wohl ein herrliches Stück!

Dichter: Nun also!

Schauspielerin: Ja, du bist ein großes Genie, Robert!

Dichter: Bei dieser Gelegenheit könntest du mir übrigens sagen, warum du vorgestern abgesagt hast. Es hat dir doch absolut gar nichts gefehlt.

Poet: Here I am. [Goes to her.]

Actress: Now, lie nice and quiet ... Pst ... don't budge.

Poet: What is the matter with you now?

Actress: I suppose you'd like to have an affair with me, wouldn't you?

Poet: That ought to be clear to you by now.

Actress: Well, lots would like to ...

Poet: But it can hardly be denied that at this particular moment I seem to have the best chance.

Actress: Come then, my cricket. I shall call you cricket from now on.

Poet: Splendid ...

Actress: Now, who am I deceiving?

Poet: Who? ... Me, perhaps ...

Actress: My poor child, you're mentally defective.

Poet: Or else someone ... whom you've never even seen ... someone you don't know ... someone who is destined for you and whom you may never find ...

Actress: For heaven's sake, stop talking fantastic nonsense.

Poet: ... Isn't it strange ... even you — and one would have thought — ... Oh, no, it would rob you of your best quality to ... come, come ... come —

* * * * *

Actress: This is much nicer than acting in idiotic plays ... don't you think so?

Poet: Well, you can be glad at least that you act in good ones now and then.

Actress: You conceited pup, I suppose you're referring to your own again?

Poet: I am indeed!

Actress: [Serious.] It really is a heavenly play!

Poet: There now, you see?

Actress: Yes, you're a great genius, Robert!

Poet: While we're on the subject, you might tell me why you refused to appear day before yesterday. There wasn't a thing the matter with you.

Schauspielerin: Nun, ich wollte dich ärgern.

Dichter: Ja warum denn? Was hab' ich dir denn getan?

Schauspielerin: Arrogant bist du gewesen.

Dichter: Wieso?

Schauspielerin: Alle im Theater finden es.

Dichter: So.

Schauspielerin: Aber ich hab' ihnen gesagt: Der Mann hat wohl ein Recht, arrogant zu sein.

Dichter: Und was haben die anderen geantwortet?

Schauspielerin: Was sollen mir denn die Leute antworten? Ich rede ja mit keinem.

Dichter: Ach so.

Schauspielerin: Sie möchten mich am liebsten alle vergiften. Aber das wird ihnen nicht gelingen.

Dichter: Denke jetzt nicht an die anderen Menschen. Freue dich lieber, daß wir hier sind und sage mir, daß du mich lieb hast.

Schauspielerin: Verlangst du noch weitere Beweise?

Dichter: Bewiesen kann das überhaupt nicht werden.

Schauspielerin: Das ist aber großartig! Was willst du denn noch?

Dichter: Wie vielen hast du es schon auf diese Art beweisen wollen ..... hast du alle geliebt?

Schauspielerin: Oh nein. Geliebt hab' ich nur einen.

Dichter: [umarmt sie.] Mein ....

Schauspielerin: Fritz.

Dichter: Ich heiße Robert. Was bin denn ich für dich, wenn du jetzt an Fritz denkst?

Schauspielerin: Du bist eine Laune.

Dichter: Gut, daß ich es weiß.

Schauspielerin: Nun sag', bist du nicht stolz?

Dichter: Ja, weshalb soll ich denn stolz sein?

Schauspielerin: Ich denke, daß du wohl einen Grund dazu hast.

Dichter: Ach deswegen.

Schauspielerin: Jawohl, deswegen, meine blasse Grille! — Nun, wie ist das mit dem Zirpen? Zirpen sie noch?

Dichter: Ununterbrochen. Hörst du's denn nicht?

Actress: I wanted to annoy you.

Poet: But what for? What have I done to you?

Actress: You were arrogant.

Poet: In what way?

Actress: Everybody in the theatre thinks you are.

Poet: I see.

Actress: But I tell them: That man has a right to be arrogant.

Poet: And what do they say?

Actress: What should they say? I don't discuss things with any of them.

Poet: I see.

Actress: They'd like nothing better than to poison me. But they won't get a chance.

Poet: Don't think of other people now. Just be happy that we're here together, and tell me that you love me.

Actress: Do you still demand proofs?

Poet: Love can't be proved, anyway.

Actress: That's magnificent! What is it that you want, then?

Poet: How many have you given proofs to in this way ... and did you love all of them?

Actress: Oh, no. I've only loved one.

Poet: [Embracing her.] My ...

Actress: Fritz.

Poet: My name is Robert. Just what do I mean to you if you're thinking of Fritz now?

Actress: You're a caprice.

Poet: I'm glad I know it, at least.

Actress: But come now, aren't you proud?

Poet: What have I got to be proud of?

Actress: I think you have some reason to be.

Poet: Oh, because of what just ...

Actress: Yes, my pale little cricket, because of that! Well, how is the chirping coming along? Are they still chirping?

Poet: Incessantly. Can't you hear it?

Schauspielerin: Freilich hör' ich. Aber das sind Frösche, mein
    Kind.

Dichter: Du irrst Dich; die quaken.

Schauspielerin: Gewiß quaken sie.

Dichter: Aber nicht hier, mein Kind, hier wird gezirpt.

Schauspielerin: Du bist wohl das eigensinnigste, was mir je
    untergekommen ist. Gib mir einen Kuß, mein Frosch!

Dichter: Bitte sehr, nenn' mich nicht so. Das macht mich
    direkt nervös.

Schauspielerin: Nun, wie soll ich dich nennen.

Dichter: Ich hab' doch einen Namen: Robert.

Schauspielerin: Ach, das ist zu dumm.

Dichter: Ich bitte dich aber, mich einfach so zu nennen, wie
    ich heiße.

Schauspielerin: Also Robert, gib mir einen Kuß ... Ah! [Sie
    küßt ihn.] Bist du jetzt zufrieden, Frosch? Hahahaha.

Dichter: Würdest du mir erlauben, mir eine Zigarette
    anzuzünden?

Schauspielerin: Gib mir auch eine. [Er nimmt die Zigarettentasche
    vom Nachtkästchen, entnimmt ihr zwei Zigaretten,
    zündet beide an, gibt ihr eine.] Du hast mir übrigens
    noch kein Wort über meine gestrige Leistung gesagt.

Dichter: Über welche Leistung?

Schauspielerin: Nun.

Dichter: Ach so. Ich war nicht im Theater.

Schauspielerin: Du beliebst wohl zu scherzen.

Dichter: Durchaus nicht. Nachdem du vorgestern abgesagt
    hast, habe ich angenommen, daß du auch gestern noch
    nicht im Vollbesitze deiner Kräfte sein würdest und da
    hab' ich lieber verzichtet.

Schauspielerin: Du hast wohl viel versäumt.

Dichter: So.

Schauspielerin: Es war sensationell. Die Menschen sind blaß
    geworden.

Dichter: Hast du das deutlich bemerkt?

Schauspielerin: Benno sagte: Kind, du hast gespielt wie eine
    Göttin.

Dichter: Hm!..... Und vorgestern noch so krank.

Actress: Certainly I hear it. But they're frogs, my pet.

Poet: You're mistaken; frogs croak.
Actress: Certainly they croak.
Poet: But not here, my child; there's only chirping done here.
Actress: You are positively the most obstinate person I ever knew. Give me a kiss, my froggy!
Poet: Please don't call me that. It makes me nervous.

Actress: Well, what shall I call you?
Poet: I have a name, haven't I? Robert.
Actress: Oh, that's so stupid.
Poet: Nevertheless, I beg you to call me simply by my own name.
Actress: Very well, then, Robert, give me a kiss ... Ah! [She kisses him.] Are you satisfied now, Froggy? Hahahaha!
Poet: Would you allow me to light a cigarette?

Actress: Give me one, too. [He takes a cigarette case from the night-table, takes out two cigarettes, lights both and gives her one.] By the way, you haven't said a word about my performance yesterday.
Poet: What performance?
Actress: Now really!
Poet: Oh, yes. But I wasn't at the theatre.
Actress: You will have your little jest.
Poet: Nothing of the sort. But as you canceled the performance day before yesterday, I quite naturally assumed that you wouldn't be in full possession of your faculties yesterday either, so I preferred to stay away.
Actress: Well, you missed a lot.
Poet: Did I?
Actress: It was sensational. The audience went pale.

Poet: Did you actually see them do it?
Actress: Benno said: My child, you acted like a goddess.

Poet: Hmmm ... and sick as a dog day before yesterday.

Schauspielerin: Jawohl; ich war es auch. Und weißt du warum? Vor Sehnsucht nach dir.

Dichter: Früher hast du mir erzählt, du wolltest mich ärgern und hast darum abgesagt.

Schauspielerin: Aber was weißt du von meiner Liebe zu dir. Dich läßt das ja alles kalt. Und ich bin schon Nächtelang im Fieber gelegen, vierzig Grad!

Dichter: Für eine Laune ist das ziemlich hoch.

Schauspielerin: Laune nennst du das? Ich sterbe vor Liebe zu dir und du nennst es Laune —?!

Dichter: Und Fritz ....?

Schauspielerin: Fritz?..... Rede mir nicht von diesem Galeerensträfling! —

Actress: Yes, indeed; I was, too. And do you know why? Out of longing for you.

Poet: A while ago you told me that you refused to play just to annoy me.

Actress: Oh, what do you know about my love for you? Everything leaves you cold. And I've been tossing about in fever night after night. A hundred and four degrees!

Poet: That's pretty high for a caprice.

Actress: A caprice, you call it? I'm dying of love for you and you call it a caprice —?!

Poet: And how about Fritz ... ?

Actress: Fritz? ... Don't talk to me about that jailbird!

9: Die Schauspielerin und der Graf

Das Schlafzimmer der Schauspielerin. Sehr üppig eingerichtet. Es ist zwölf Uhr mittags; die Rouleaux sind noch herunter gelassen; auf dem Nachtkästchen brennt eine Kerze, die Schauspielerin liegt noch in ihrem Himmelbett. Auf der Decke liegen zahlreiche Zeitungen.

Der Graf tritt ein in der Uniform eines Dragonerrittmeisters. Er bleibt an der Tür stehen. —

Schauspielerin: Ah, Herr Graf.
Graf: Die Frau Mama hat mir erlaubt, sonst wär' ich nicht —

Schauspielerin: Bitte, treten Sie nur näher.
Graf: Küß' die Hand. Pardon — wenn man von der Straßen hereinkommt .... ich seh' nämlich noch rein gar nichts. So .... da wären wir ja [am Bett.] Küß die Hand.
Schauspielerin: Nehmen Sie Platz, Herr Graf.
Graf: Frau Mama sagte mir, Fräulein sind unpäßlich .... Wird doch hoffentlich nichts ernstes sein.
Schauspielerin: Nichts ernstes? Ich bin dem Tode nahe gewesen!
Graf: Um Gotteswillen, wie ist denn das möglich?
Schauspielerin: Es ist jedenfalls sehr freundlich, daß Sie sich zu mir bemühen.
Graf: Dem Tode nahe! Und gestern Abend haben Sie noch gespielt wie eine Göttin.
Schauspielerin: Es war wohl ein großer Triumph.
Graf: Kolossal!.... Die Leute waren auch alle hingerissen. Und von mir will ich gar nicht reden.
Schauspielerin: Ich danke für die schönen Blumen.
Graf: Aber bitt' Sie Fräulein.

9: The Actress and the Count

The actress' bedroom. Very luxuriously furnished. It is high noon; the blinds are still down; a candle is still burning on the night-table, and the Actress is still lying on her canopied bed. Innumerable newspapers are strewn over the bedspread.

The count enters, dressed in the uniform of an Officer of the Dragoons. He remains standing in the doorway.

Actress: Ah, Count!

Count: I have your mother's permission, otherwise I would not have —

Actress: Come right in, won't you?

Count: Thank you. Excuse me — coming right in from the street, it's very hard to see anything. Ah ... there we are ... [At the bed.] How do you do?

Actress: Do sit down, Count.

Count: Your mother told me you were indisposed ... Nothing serious, I hope.

Actress: Nothing serious? I nearly died.

Count: Good heavens, how was that possible?

Actress: Anyway, it's terribly nice of you to bother about me.

Count: Nearly died! And yesterday you acted like a goddess!

Actress: It was quite a triumph, I think.

Count: Magnificent! ... The audience was absolutely carried away ... not to speak of myself.

Actress: Thank you for the lovely flowers.

Count: Don't mention it, please.

Schauspielerin: [mit den Augen auf einen großen Blumenkorb weisend, der auf einem kleinen Tischchen auf dem Fenster steht.] Hier stehen sie.

Graf: Sie sind gestern förmlich überschüttet worden mit Blumen und Kränzen.

Schauspielerin: Das liegt noch alles in meiner Garderobe. Nur Ihren Korb habe ich mit nach Hause gebracht.

Graf: [küßt ihr die Hand.] Das ist lieb von Ihnen. [Schauspielerin nimmt die seine plötzlich und küßt sie.] Aber Fräulein.

Schauspielerin: Erschrecken Sie nicht, Herr Graf, das verpflichtet Sie zu gar nichts.

Graf: Sie sind ein sonderbares Wesen .... rätselhaft könnte man fast sagen. — [Pause.]

Schauspielerin: Das Fräulein Birken ist wohl leichter aufzulösen.

Graf: Ja die kleine Birken ist kein Problem, obzwar .... ich kenne sie ja auch nur oberflächlich.

Schauspielerin: Ha!

Graf: Sie können mir's glauben. Aber Sie sind ein Problem. Danach hab' ich immer Sehnsucht gehabt. Es ist mir eigentlich ein großer Genuß entgangen, dadurch, daß ich Sie gestern .... das erste Mal spielen gesehen habe.

Schauspielerin: Ist das möglich?

Graf: Ja. Schauen Sie, Fräulein, es ist so schwer mit dem Theater. Ich bin gewöhnt, spät zu dinieren ..... also wenn man dann hinkommt, ist's beste vorbei. Ist's nicht wahr?

Schauspielerin: So werden Sie eben von jetzt an früher essen.

Graf: Ja, ich hab' auch schon daran gedacht. Oder gar nicht. Es ist ja wirklich kein Vergnügen, das Dinieren.

Schauspielerin: Was kennen Sie jugendlicher Greis eigentlich noch für ein Vergnügen?

Graf: Das frag' ich mich selber manchmal! Aber ein Greis bin ich nicht. Es muß einen anderen Grund haben.

Schauspielerin: Glauben Sie?

Graf: Ja. Der Lulu sagt beispielsweise, ich bin ein Philosoph. Wissen Sie, Fräulein, er meint, ich denk' zu viel nach.

Schauspielerin: Ja .... denken, das ist das Unglück.

Actress: [Turning her eyes in the direction of a huge basket of flowers standing on a little table by the window.] There they are.

Count: Last night you were literally showered with flowers and wreaths.

Actress: They're all in my dressing-room still. I took only your basket home with me.

Count: [Kissing her hand.] That was charming of you. [Actress takes his hand suddenly and kisses it.] But, my dear ...

Actress: Don't be alarmed, Count, that doesn't obligate you in any way!

Count: You are an extraordinary creature ... one might almost say, puzzling — [Pause.]

Actress: Miss Birken is easier to solve, I imagine.

Count: Yes, Little Miss Birken is no problem ... although I really know her only superficially.

Actress: Ha!

Count: You may believe me. But you're a distinct problem. I've always had a passion for problems. When I saw you for the first time last night, I realized what a great pleasure I had missed in not seeing you act before.

Actress: Was it really the first time you'd seen me?

Count: Yes. You see, it's very difficult for me to go to the theatre. I'm used to dining late ... so that when one finally gets there the best part's over. Isn't that so?

Actress: You'd better dine earlier from now on.

Count: Yes, I've been thinking of that. Or not dining at all. It's really not much pleasure, dining.

Actress: Is there any pleasure yet left for you, you youthful dotard?

Count: I wonder about that myself, sometimes! But I'm not a dotard. There must be some other reason.

Actress: You think so?

Count: Yes. For instance, Louis says I'm a philosopher. He means, you see, that I think too much.

Actress: Yes ... it's disastrous to think.

Graf: Ich hab' zu viel Zeit, d'rum denk' ich nach. Bitt' Sie, Fräulein, schauen S', ich hab' mir gedacht, wenn s' mich nach Wien transferieren, wird's besser. Da gibt's Zerstreuung, Anregung. Aber es ist im Grund doch nicht anders als da oben.

Schauspielerin: Wo ist denn das da oben?

Graf: Na, da unten, wissen S' Fräulein, in Ungarn, in die Nester, wo ich meistens in Garnison war.

Schauspielerin: Ja, was haben Sie denn in Ungarn gemacht?

Graf: Na, wie ich sag', Fräulein, Dienst.

Schauspielerin: Ja warum sind Sie denn so lang in Ungarn geblieben?

Graf: Ja, das kommt so.

Schauspielerin: Da muß man ja wahnsinnig werden.

Graf: Warum denn? Zu tun hat man eigentlich mehr wie da. Wissen S' Fräulein, Rekruten ausbilden, Remonten reiten .... und dann ist's nicht so arg mit der Gegend, wie man sagt. Es ist schon ganz was schönes, die Tiefebene — und so ein Sonnenuntergang, es ist schade, daß ich kein Maler bin, ich hab' mir manchmal gedacht, wenn ich ein Maler wär', tät' ich's malen. Einen haben wir gehabt beim Regiment, einen jungen Splany, der hat's können. — Aber was erzähl' ich Ihnen da für fade G'schichten, Fräulein.

Schauspielerin: Oh bitte, ich amüsiere mich königlich.

Graf: Wissen S' Fräulein, mit Ihnen kann man plaudern, das hat mir der Lulu schon g'sagt, und das ist's, was man selten find't.

Schauspielerin: Nun freilich, in Ungarn.

Graf: Aber in Wien grad' so! Die Menschen sind überall dieselben; da wo mehr sind, ist halt das Gedräng' größer, das ist der ganze Unterschied. Sagen S' Fräulein, haben Sie die Menschen eigentlich gern?

Schauspielerin: Gern —?? Ich hasse sie! Ich kann keine seh'n! Ich seh' auch nie jemanden. Ich bin immer allein, dieses Haus betritt niemand.

Graf: Seh'n S', das hab' ich mir gedacht, daß Sie eigentlich eine Menschenfeindin sind. Bei der Kunst muß das oft

Count: I have too much time, that's why I think so much.
You see, it's this way, Madame, I thought that things
would be better if they transferred me to Vienna.
There's distraction here, and excitement. But when you
come right down to it, it's no different than up there.

Actress: Up where?

Count: You know, Madame, down there, in Hungary, in
those rotten holes where our garrisons were stationed.

Actress: Well, what did you do in Hungary?

Count: What I told you, Madame, military service.

Actress: But why did you stay such a long time in Hungary?

Count: Oh well, it just happened so.

Actress: It must be enough to drive one mad.

Count: How so? Actually, there's more to do there than here.
You know, what with drilling recruits, remount riding
... and then, the country isn't as bad as they say. It's
really quite beautiful, that prairie-land — and as for the
sunsets there, it's really a shame I'm not a painter. I've
often thought if I were a painter I'd surely paint them.
There was a fellow in our regiment, young Splany, he
could have done it. — But what am I telling you all
these boring things for?

Actress: Oh, don't say that, I'm being royally entertained.

Count: You know, Madame, it's so easy to chat with you.
Louis said so too; and it's a very hard thing to find.

Actress: In Hungary, I can imagine.

Count: But it's just as hard in Vienna! People everywhere
are alike; the only difference is that there's more of a
crowd where more of 'em are. Incidentally, do you like
people, Madame?

Actress: Like them? I loathe them! I can hardly bear to see
them! I don't see anyone ever, as a matter of fact. I'm
always alone, there's never a soul in this house.

Count: Ah, I thought you were a hater of society. Artistic
people are often that way. When one moves in higher

vorkommen. Wenn man so in den höheren Regionen .... na, Sie haben's gut, Sie wissen doch wenigstens, warum Sie leben!

Schauspielerin: Wer sagt Ihnen das? Ich habe keine Ahnung, wozu ich lebe!

Graf: Ich bitt' Sie, Fräulein, — berühmt — gefeiert —

Schauspielerin: Ist das vielleicht ein Glück?

Graf: Glück? Bitt' Sie Fräulein, Glück giebt's nicht. Überhaupt gerade die Sachen, von denen am meisten g'redt wird, giebt's nicht ... z. B. Liebe. Das ist auch so 'was.

Schauspielerin: Da haben Sie wohl recht.

Graf: Genuß .... Rausch .... also gut, da läßt sich nichts sagen .... das ist 'was sicheres. Jetzt genieße ich, ... gut, weiß ich, ich genieß'. Oder ich bin berauscht, schön. Das ist auch sicher. Und ist's vorbei, so ist es halt vorbei.

Schauspielerin: [groß.] Es ist vorbei!

Graf: Aber sobald man sich nicht, wie soll ich mich denn ausdrücken, sobald man sich nicht dem Moment hingiebt, also an später denkt oder an früher .... na, ist es doch gleich aus. Später .... ist traurig .... früher ist ungewiß .... mit einem Wort .... man wird nur konfus. Hab' ich nicht recht?

Schauspielerin: [nickt mit großen Augen.] Sie haben wohl den Sinn erfaßt.

Graf: Und sehen S', Fräulein, wenn einem das einmal klar geworden ist, ist's ganz egal, ob man in Wien lebt oder in der Pußta oder in Steinamanger. Schaun S' zum Beispiel .... wo darf ich denn die Kappen hinlegen? So, ich dank' schön .... wovon haben wir denn nur gesprochen?

Schauspielerin: Von Steinamanger.

Graf: Richtig. Also wie ich sag', der Unterschied ist nicht groß. Ob ich am Abend im Kasino sitz' oder im Klub, ist doch alles eins.

Schauspielerin: Und wie verhält sich denn das mit der Liebe?

Graf: Wenn man d'ran glaubt, ist immer eine da, die einen gern' hat.

Schauspielerin: Zum Beispiel das Fräulein Birken.

realms ... well, you're lucky, at least you know why you're living!

Actress: Who says I do? I haven't the faintest idea what I'm living for!

Count: But, surely, Madame — fame — honors —

Actress: Is that supposed to be happiness?

Count: Happiness? There's no such thing, Madame. It's the very things that people talk about most that don't exist ... for instance, Love. That's one of them.

Actress: You may be right.

Count: Pleasure ... intoxication ... granted, they're not to be denied ... they're facts. I am enjoying something ... good, I know that I'm enjoying it. Or I'm drunk, good again. That's definite too. And when it's over, it's over and done with.

Actress: [Grandly.] Over and done with!

Count: But if — how shall I express it — if one doesn't surrender to the moment alone, but thinks of the past or the future — well, you're done for, either way. The past is sad ... the future is uncertain ... in a word, nothing but confusion. Isn't that so?

Actress: [Nodding, with wide eyes.] You've hit the nail on the head.

Count: So you see, Madame, once that's become clear it makes absolutely no difference whether one lives in Vienna or in the Hungarian plains or in Kalamazoo. Or, for instance ... I wonder where I laid my cap? Ah, thank you ... what were we saying?

Actress: Kalamazoo.

Count: Oh yes. Well, as I said, there's not much difference. It's the same thing whether I sit in the Casino or in the Club.

Actress: And what has that to do with love?

Count: If you believe in love, you'll always find someone to love you.

Actress: Miss Birken, for instance.

Graf: Ich weiß wirklich nicht, Fräulein, warum Sie immer auf die kleine Birken zu reden kommen.

Schauspielerin: Das ist doch Ihre Geliebte.

Graf: Wer sagt denn das?

Schauspielerin: Jeder Mensch weiß das.

Graf: Nur ich nicht, es ist merkwürdig.

Schauspielerin: Sie haben doch ihretwegen ein Duell gehabt!

Graf: Vielleicht bin ich sogar tot geschossen worden und hab's gar nicht bemerkt.

Schauspielerin: Nun, Herr Graf, Sie sind ein Ehrenmann. Setzen Sie sich näher.

Graf: Bin so frei.

Schauspielerin: Hierher [sie zieht ihn an sich, fährt ihm mit der Hand durch die Haare.] Ich hab' gewußt, daß Sie heute kommen werden!

Graf: Wieso denn?

Schauspielerin: Ich hab' es bereits gestern im Theater gewußt.

Graf: Haben Sie mich denn von der Bühne aus gesehen?

Schauspielerin: Aber Mann! Haben Sie denn nicht bemerkt, daß ich nur für Sie spiele?

Graf: Wie ist das denn möglich?

Schauspielerin: Ich bin ja so geflogen, wie ich Sie in der ersten Reihe sitzen sah!

Graf: Geflogen? Meinetwegen? Ich hab' keine Ahnung gehabt, daß Sie mich bemerken!

Schauspielerin: Sie können einen auch mit Ihrer Vornehmheit zur Verzweiflung bringen.

Graf: Ja Fräulein ....

Schauspielerin: »Ja Fräulein«!... So schnallen Sie doch wenigstens Ihren Säbel ab!

Graf: Wenn es erlaubt ist. [Schnallt ihn ab, lehnt ihn ans Bett.]

Schauspielerin: Und gib mir endlich einen Kuß. [Graf küßt sie, sie läßt ihn nicht los.] Dich hätte ich auch lieber nie erblicken sollen.

Graf: Es ist doch besser so! —

Schauspielerin: Herr Graf, Sie sind ein Poseur!

Graf: Ich — warum denn?

Count: I really don't know why you keep referring to little Miss Birken all the time, Madame.

Actress: She's your sweetheart, isn't she?

Count: Who said so?

Actress: Everybody knows it.

Count: Except me. That's remarkable.

Actress: But you fought a duel because of her!

Count: Maybe I was shot dead and didn't notice it.

Actress: I see you're a man of honor, Count. Come, sit a little nearer.

Count: If I may ...

Actress: Over here. [She draws him to her, runs her fingers through his hair.] I knew you would come today!

Count: How so?

Actress: In fact, I knew it last night in the theatre.

Count: Then you did see me from the stage?

Actress: My dear man! Didn't you notice that I was acting only for you?

Count: I can't believe it!

Actress: I was so flustered when I saw you sitting in the first row!

Count: Flustered? On my account? Why, I had no idea that you even noticed me.

Actress: You're enough to drive one to despair with that superior manner of yours.

Count: But, Madame ...

Actress: "But, Madame!" ... Really, you might at least unbuckle your sabre!

Count: If I may. [Unbuckles sabre and lays it on bed.]

Actress: And isn't it about time you kissed me? [Count kisses her, she doesn't release him.] I should never have laid eyes on you.

Count: But surely it's better as it is!

Actress: Count, I'm afraid you're a poseur, after all!

Count: I? But why?

Schauspielerin: Was glauben Sie, wie glücklich wär' mancher, wenn er an Ihrer Stelle sein dürfte!

Graf: Ich bin sehr glücklich.

Schauspielerin: Nun, ich dachte, es gibt kein Glück. Wie schaust du mich denn an? Ich glaube Sie haben Angst vor mir, Herr Graf!

Graf: Ich sag's ja, Fräulein, Sie sind ein Problem.

Schauspielerin: Ach laß' du mich in Frieden mit der Philosophie .... komm' zu mir. Und jetzt bitt' mich um irgend 'was .... du kannst alles haben, was du willst. Du bist zu schön.

Graf: Also ich bitte um die Erlaubnis [ihre Hand küssend], daß ich heute abends wiederkommen darf.

Schauspielerin: Heut Abend .... ich spiele ja.

Graf: Nach dem Theater.

Schauspielerin: Um was anderes bittest du nicht?

Graf: Um alles andere werde ich nach dem Theater bitten.

Schauspielerin: [verletzt.] Da kannst du lange bitten, du elender Poseur.

Graf: Ja schauen Sie, oder schau, wir sind doch bis jetzt so aufrichtig miteinander gewesen ... Ich fände das alles viel schöner am Abend nach dem Theater ... gemütlicher als jetzt, wo ... ich hab' immer so die Empfindung, als könnte die Thür aufgeh'n ....

Schauspielerin: Die geht nicht von außen auf.

Graf: Schau' ich find', man soll sich nicht leichtsinnig von vornherein 'was verderben, was möglicherweise sehr schön sein könnte.

Schauspielerin: Möglicherweise!....

Graf: In der Früh', wenn ich die Wahrheit sagen soll, find' ich die Liebe gräßlich.

Schauspielerin: Nun — du bist wohl das irrsinnigste, was mir je vorgekommen ist!

Graf: Ich red' ja nicht von beliebigen Frauenzimmern .... schließlich im allgemeinen ist's ja egal. Aber Frauen wie du ... nein, du kannst mich hundertmal einen Narren heißen. Aber Frauen wie du .... nimmt man nicht vor dem Frühstück zu sich. Und so .... weißt .... so ....

Actress: Don't you think that many would be extremely happy if they were in your place?

Count: I'm very happy.

Actress: Ha, I thought there was no such thing as happiness! How you look at me! I do believe you're afraid of me, Count!

Count: I told you you were a problem, didn't I?

Actress: Oh, spare me your philosophy ... come to me. And now ask me for something ... you can have anything you want. You're so handsome.

Count: Well then, I beg you [Kisses her hand] to let me come again tonight.

Actress: Tonight? But I'm performing.

Count: After the theatre.

Actress: And you want nothing else?

Count: I'll ask for everything else after the theatre.

Actress: [Hurt.] You'll ask a long time, you miserable poseur.

Count: But, please, don't you see, you must see, we've been so open with each other so far ... it would all be so much nicer at night, after the theatre ... much cosier than now, when ... I have the feeling constantly as if the door were about to open ...

Actress: The door can't open from the outside.

Count: But you see, I feel that one shouldn't plunge into something frivolously and spoil what might be a very beautiful thing.

Actress: Might be! . .

Count: To be candid, I find love simply hideous in the morning.

Actress: Really — you're the maddest thing I've ever come across!

Count: I'm not speaking of the common run of women ... after all, it's all the same, in the aggregate. But women like you ... call me a fool, if you will ... women like you must not be made love to before breakfast. And therefore ... you see ...

Schauspielerin: Gott, was bist du süß!

Graf: Siehst du das ein, was ich g'sagt hab', nicht wahr. Ich stell mir das so vor —

Schauspielerin: Nun, wie stellst du dir das vor?

Graf: Ich denk' mir ..... ich wart' nach dem Theater auf dich in ein' Wagen, dann fahren wir zusammen also irgendwohin soupieren —

Schauspielerin: Ich bin nicht das Fräulein Birken.

Graf: Das hab' ich ja nicht gesagt. Ich find' nur, zu allem g'hört Stimmung. Ich komm' immer erst beim Souper in Stimmung. Das ist dann das schönste, wenn man so vom Souper zusamm' nach Haus fahrt, dann ....

Schauspielerin: Was ist dann?

Graf: Also dann ... liegt das in der Entwicklung der Dinge.

Schauspielerin: Setz' dich doch näher. Näher.

Graf: [sich aufs Bett setzend.] Ich muß schon sagen, aus den Polstern kommt so ein ... Reseda ist das — nicht?

Schauspielerin: Es ist sehr heiß hier, findest du nicht? [Graf neigt sich und küßt ihren Hals.] Oh, Herr Graf, das ist ja gegen Ihr Programm.

Graf: Wer sagt denn das? Ich hab' kein Programm. [Schauspielerin zieht ihn an sich.] Es ist wirklich heiß.

Schauspielerin: Findest du? Und so dunkel, wie wenn's Abend wär'..... [reißt ihn an sich.] Es ist Abend .... es ist Nacht .... Mach' die Augen zu, wenn's dir zu licht ist. Komm!... Komm!.... [Graf wehrt sich nicht mehr.]

* * * * *

Schauspielerin: Nun, wie ist das jetzt mit der Stimmung, du Poseur?

Graf: Du bist ein kleiner Teufel.

Schauspielerin: Was ist das für ein Ausdruck?

Graf: Na, also ein Engel.

Schauspielerin: Und du hättest Schauspieler werden sollen! Wahrhaftig! Du kennst die Frauen! Und weißt du, was ich jetzt tun werde?

Graf: Nun?

Schauspielerin: Ich werde dir sagen, daß ich dich nie wiedersehen will.

Actress: God, aren't you sweet!

Count: You see what I mean, don't you? Imagine it like this —

Actress: Well, how do you imagine it?

Count: I had the idea. I'd wait for you after the theatre in my car, then we'd drive somewhere for supper —

Actress: I'm not Miss Birken, you know.

Count: I didn't say you were. Only it seems to me that atmosphere — mood — is important to everything. I'm never in the right mood till after supper. There's nothing more delightful than driving home together after supper, and then ...

Actress: Then what?

Count: Well, then ... events can take their natural course.

Actress: Sit closer. Closer.

Count: [Sitting on the bed.] There's a ... an aroma of mignonette coming out of your pillows, isn't there?

Actress: Don't you find it very hot in this room? [Count bends over and kisses her neck.] Oh, Count, that's not according to your program.

Count: Why do you say that? I have no program. [Actress draws him to her.] It really is hot.

Actress: Do you think so? And it's dark, too, almost as dark as night. [Pulls him down to her.] It is evening ... it is night ... close your eyes if it's too light for you. Come! ... Come! [Count resists no longer.]

* * * * *

Actress: Well, how is your mood now, poseur?

Count: You're a little devil.

Actress: What a thing to call me!

Count: Well then, angel.

Actress: You should have been an actor! Really! You understand women! Do you know what I shall do now?

Count: Well?

Actress: I shall tell you that I'll never see you again.

Graf: Warum denn?

Schauspielerin: Nein, nein. Du bist mir zu gefährlich! Du machst ja ein Weib toll. Jetzt stehst du plötzlich vor mir, als wär' nichts gescheh'n.

Graf: Aber .....

Schauspielerin: Ich bitte sich zu erinnern, Herr Graf, ich bin soeben Ihre Geliebte gewesen.

Graf: Ich werd's nie vergessen!

Schauspielerin: Und wie ist das mit heute Abend?

Graf: Wie meinst du das?

Schauspielerin: Nun — du wolltest mich ja nach dem Theater erwarten?

Graf: Ja, also gut, zum Beispiel übermorgen.

Schauspielerin: Was heißt das, übermorgen? Es war doch von heute die Rede.

Graf: Das hätte keinen rechten Sinn.

Schauspielerin: Du Greis!

Graf: Du verstehst mich nicht recht. Ich mein' das mehr, was, wie soll ich mich ausdrücken, was die Seele anbelangt.

Schauspielerin: Was geht mich deine Seele an?

Graf: Glaub' mir, sie gehört mit dazu. Ich halte das für eine falsche Ansicht, daß man das so voneinander trennen kann.

Schauspielerin: Laß mich mit deiner Philosophie in Frieden. Wenn ich das haben will, lese ich Bücher.

Graf: Aus Büchern lernt man ja doch nie.

Schauspielerin: Das ist wohl wahr! Drum sollst du mich heut' Abend erwarten. Wegen der Seele werden wir uns schon einigen, du Schurke!

Graf: Also wenn du erlaubst, so werde ich mit meinem Wagen .....

Schauspielerin: Hier in meiner Wohnung wirst du mich erwarten —

Graf: ..... Nach dem Theater.

Schauspielerin: Natürlich. [Er schnallt den Säbel um.] Was machst du denn da?

Graf: Ich denke, es ist Zeit, daß ich geh'. Für einen Anstandsbesuch bin ich doch eigentlich schon ein bissel lang' geblieben.

Count: But why?

Actress: No, never. You're too dangerous for me! You drive a woman mad. You sit there now as if nothing at all had happened.

Count: But ...

Actress: Kindly remember, Count, that I have just been your belovèd!

Count: I shall never forget it!

Actress: And now how about tonight?

Count: What do you mean?

Actress: Well — you were going to wait for me after the theatre.

Count: Very well then, how about day after tomorrow, say?

Actress: What do you mean, day after tomorrow? We were talking about tonight.

Count: There wouldn't be any sense in that.

Actress: Old dotard!

Count: You don't understand me. It's the — how shall I say it — the spiritual aspect of the thing that I'm referring to.

Actress: What do I care about your spirit?

Count: Believe me, that belongs to it too. It's a fallacy to think that one can separate the one from the other.

Actress: Oh, stop philosophizing. When I want philosophy I read books.

Count: One can never really learn from books.

Actress: That's true enough! And that's why you should wait for me tonight. And as for the spiritual aspect, we'll attend to that alright, you rascal!

Count: Well, then, with your permission I'll have my car ...

Actress: You'll wait for me here, at home —

Count: ... After the theatre.

Actress: Of course. [He buckles on his sabre.] What are you doing?

Count: I think it's time for me to go. I've stayed a bit too long for a social call as it is.

Schauspielerin: Nun, heut abend soll es kein Anstandsbesuch werden.

Graf: Glaubst du?

Schauspielerin: Dafür laß nur mich sorgen. Und jetzt gieb mir noch einen Kuß, mein kleiner Philosoph. So, du Verführer, du .... süßes Kind, du Seelenverkäufer, Du Iltis .... du .... [Nachdem sie ihn ein paarmal heftig geküßt, stößt sie ihn heftig von sich.] Herr Graf, es war mir eine große Ehre!

Graf: Ich küß' die Hand, Fräulein! [Bei der Thür.] Auf Wiederschaun'.

Schauspielerin: Adieu, Steinamanger!

Actress: Well, it won't be a social call tonight.

Count: You think not?

Actress: Let me take care of that. And now give me one more kiss, my little philosopher. There, you seducer, you ... sweet child, you barterer of souls, you ... [After a few ardent kisses, she pushes him forcibly from her.] ... Count, it has been a great honor!

Count: I salute you, Madame! [At the door.] Good day.

Actress: Goodbye, Kalamazoo!

10: Der Graf und die Dirne

Morgen, gegen sechs Uhr.

Ein ärmliches Zimmer; einfenstrig, die gelblich-schmutzigen Rouletten sind heruntergelassen. Verschlissene grünliche Vorhänge. Eine Kommode, auf der ein paar Photographien stehen und ein auffallend geschmackloser, billiger Damenhut liegt. Hinter dem Spiegel billige japanische Fächer. Auf dem Tisch, der mit einem rötlichen Schutztuch überzogen ist, steht eine Petroleumlampe, die schwach brenzlich brennt; papierener, gelber Lampenschirm, daneben ein Krug, in dem ein Rest von Bier ist, und ein halb geleertes Glas. Auf dem Boden neben dem Bett liegen unordentlich Frauenkleider, als wenn sie eben rasch abgeworfen worden wären.

Im Bett liegt schlafend die Dirne; sie atmet ruhig. — Auf dem Divan, völlig angekleidet, liegt der Graf, im Drapp-Überzieher; der Hut liegt zu Häupten des Divans auf dem Boden.

Graf: [bewegt sich, reibt die Augen, erhebt sich rasch, bleibt sitzen, schaut um sich.] Ja, wie bin ich denn .... Ah so .... Also bin ich richtig mit dem Frauenzimmer nach Haus .... [Er steht rasch auf, sieht ihr Bett.] Da liegt s' ja .... Was einem noch alles in meinem Alter passieren kann. Ich hab' keine Idee, haben s' mich da heraufgetragen? Nein .... ich hab' ja geseh'n — ich komm in das Zimmer .... ja .... da bin ich noch wach gewesen oder wach worden .... oder .... oder ist vielleicht nur, daß mich das Zimmer an was erinnert?.... Meiner Seel', na ja .... gestern hab' ich's halt g'seh'n .... [sieht auf die Uhr.] was! gestern, vor ein paar Stunden — Aber ich hab's g'wußt, daß

10: The Count and the Tart

Morning, about six o'clock.

A poorly furnished room with one window, over which dirty yellowish shades are pulled down. Faded greenish curtains. A chest of drawers. On it are a few photographs and a woman's hat, cheap and atrocious in taste. Garish Japanese fans are stuck in the mirror. On the table, covered with a reddish cloth, stands an oil-lamp with a yellow paper lampshade, burning dimly and smokily; a pitcher with some remnants of beer in it, and a half-empty glass. On the floor next to the bed a woman's clothes are lying in disorder, as if they had been hastily thrown off.

The tart is lying asleep in bed, breathing quietly. On the sofa, fully dressed and wearing a light overcoat, lies the Count. His hat is on the floor at the head of the sofa.

Count: [Stirs, rubs his eyes, sits up quickly, looks about him] Where am I? ... Oh yes... . So I did go home with the woman after all... . [Gets up, sees her bed.] There she lies... . God, the things that can happen to a man of my age. I haven't the faintest idea, did they carry me up here, I wonder? No... . I remember seeing — I came into the room ... yes ... I was still awake then, or had just waked up ... or ... is it just that this room reminds me of something? ... 'pon my soul, yes... . I did see it all yesterday... . [Looks at his watch.] Yesterday hell! ... a few hours ago — But I knew something was bound to

'was passieren muß ..... ich hab's g'spürt .... wie ich
ang'fangen hab' zu trinken gestern, hab' ich's g'spürt,
daß .... Und was ist denn passiert?..... Also nichts .....
Oder ist was .....? Meiner Seel .... seit .... also seit zehn
Jahren ist mir so 'was nicht vor'kommen, daß ich nicht
weiß .... Also kurz und gut, ich war halt b'soffen. Wenn
ich nur wüßt', von wann an .... Also das weiß ich noch
ganz genau, wie ich in das Hurenkaffeehaus hinein bin
mit dem Lulu und .... nein, nein .... vom Sacher sind wir
ja noch weg'gangen .... und dann auf dem Weg ist schon
.... Ja richtig, ich bin ja in meinem Wagen g'fahren mit'm
Lulu .... Was zerbrich ich mir denn viel den Kopf. Ist ja
egal. Schau'n wir, daß wir weiterkommen. [Steht auf.
Die Lampe wackelt.] Oh! [Sieht auf die Schlafende.]
Die hat halt einen g'sunden Schlaf. Ich weiß zwar von
gar nix — aber ich werd' ihr 's Geld aufs Nachtkastel
legen .... und Servus .... [Er steht vor ihr, sieht sie lange
an.] Wenn man nicht wüßt', was sie ist! [Betrachtet
sie lang.] Ich hab' viel kennt, die haben nicht einmal
im Schlafen so tugendhaft ausg'seh'n. Meiner Seel' ....
also der Lulu möcht' wieder sagen, ich philosophier',
aber es ist wahr, der Schlaf macht auch schon gleich,
kommt mir vor; — wie der Herr Bruder, also der Tod
.... Hm, ich möcht' nur wissen, ob .... Nein, daran müßt'
ich mich ja erinnern .... Nein, nein, ich bin gleich da
auf den Divan herg'fallen .... und nichts is g'schehn
.... Es ist unglaublich, wie sich manchmal alle Weiber
ähnlich schauen .... Na geh'n wir. [Er will gehen.] Ja
richtig. [Er nimmt die Brieftasche und ist eben daran
eine Banknote herauszunehmen.]

Dirne: [wacht auf.] Na .... wer ist denn in aller Früh —?
[Erkennt ihn.]. Servus, Bubi!

Graf: Guten Morgen. Hast gut g'schlafen?

Dirne: [reckt sich.] Ah, komm her. Pussi geben.

Graf: [beugt sich zu ihr herab, besinnt sich, wieder fort.] Ich
hab' grad' fortgehen wollen ....

Dirne: Fortgeh'n?

Graf: Es ist wirklich die höchste Zeit.

happen... . I felt it coming... . When I began drinking yesterday I felt that ... but what did happen, anyway? ... Nothing, maybe... . Or did it ... ? 'Pon my soul ... since ... well, for ten years this sort of thing hasn't happened to me, not knowing what... . Oh well, the whole point is that I was good and drunk... . If only I knew from when on... . I do remember perfectly well going into that dive with Louis ... no, no ... we left Sacher's together ... and then, on the way over already... . Yes, that's right, I was riding in my car with Louis... . What's the use of racking my brains over it, anyway. What's the odds? ... The main thing is to get out. [Stands up. The lamp shakes.] Oh! [Looks at the sleeping woman.] She sleeps soundly enough. I don't remember a damn thing — but I'll leave some money on the night-table ... and beat it... . [Stands looking at her for quite a while.] If one didn't know what she was ... ! [Studies her closely.] I've seen a lot of women that didn't look as virtuous, even in their sleep. 'Pon my soul... . Louis would probably say I was philosophizing again, but it's perfectly true. Sleep seems to be a leveler too — like its venerable brother, Death... . Hm, I'd just like to know whether ... no, I would have remembered that ... no, no, I collapsed on the sofa right away ... and nothing happened... . It's incredible how all women look alike sometimes ... well, let's move along. [He starts to go.] Oh yes ... [Takes out his wallet and extracts a bill from it.

Tart: [wakes up.]Well ... who's here so early —? [Recognizes him.] Hello, kid!

Count: Good morning. Sleep well?

Tart: [Stretching.] Aw, come here. Give us a kiss.

Count: [Bends over her, hesitates, draws back.] I was just going ...

Tart: Going?

Count: It's really high time I did.

Dirne: So willst du fortgeh'n?

Graf: [fast verlegen.] So ....

Dirne: Na, Servus; kommst halt ein anderesmal.

Graf: Ja, grüß dich Gott. Na, willst nicht das Handerl geben? [Dirne gibt die Hand aus der Decke hervor. Graf nimmt die Hand und küßt sie mechanisch, bemerkt es, lacht.] Wie einer Prinzessin. Übrigens, wenn man nur ....

Dirne: Was schaust mich denn so an?

Graf: Wenn man nur das Kopferl sieht, wie jetzt .... beim Aufwachen sieht doch eine jede unschuldig aus .... meiner Seel, alles mögliche könnt' man sich einbilden, wenn's nicht so nach Petroleum stinken möcht' ....

Dirne: Ja, mit der Lampen ist immer ein G'frett.

Graf: Wie alt bist denn eigentlich?

Dirne: Na, was glaubst?

Graf: Vierundzwanzig.

Dirne: Ja freilich.

Graf: Bist schon älter?

Dirne: Ins zwanzigste geh' i.

Graf: Und wie lang bist du schon ....

Dirne: Bei dem G'schäft bin i ein Jahr!

Graf: Da hast du aber früh ang'fangen.

Dirne: Besser zu früh als zu spät.

Graf: [setzt sich aufs Bett.] Sag' mir einmal, bist du eigentlich glücklich?

Dirne: Was?

Graf: Also ich mein', geht's dir gut?

Dirne: Oh, mir geht's alleweil gut.

Graf: So .... Sag', ist dir noch nie eing'fallen, daß du was anderes werden könntest?

Dirne: Was soll i denn werden?

Graf: Also .... Du bist doch wirklich ein hübsches Mädel. Du könntest doch z. B. einen Geliebten haben.

Dirne: Meinst vielleicht, ich hab' kein?

Graf: Ja, das weiß ich — ich mein' aber einen, weißt einen, der dich aushalt, daß du nicht mit einem jeden zu geh'n brauchst.

Tart: You're going away just like this?

Count: [Almost embarrassed.] Like this?

Tart: Well, so long then, see you another time.

Count: Yes, and good luck to you. How about shaking hands? [Tart holds out her hand from the covers. Count takes it and kisses it mechanically, notices the fact, laughs.] Just like a princess. As a matter of fact, when one only ...

Tart: Why do you look at me that way?

Count: When one only sees the head, as it is now ... when they're just waking up everyone looks innocent, anyway ... 'pon my soul, one could imagine oneself almost anywhere, if only it didn't stink of kerosene ...

Tart: Yes, that lamp's always on the blink.

Count: How old are you, anyway?

Tart: Well, what do you think?

Count: Twenty-four.

Tart: You don't say.

Count: Older than that?

Tart: Going on twenty.

Count: And how long have you been ...

Tart: I've been in business for one year.

Count: You started early, alright.

Tart: Better too soon than too late.

Count: [Sitting on the bed.] Tell me, are you really happy?

Tart: What?

Count: I mean, are you getting along all right?

Tart: Oh, I get along good enough.

Count: I see. But hasn't it ever occurred to you that you might be doing something else?

Tart: What else could I be doing?

Count: Well ... you're really a pretty girl, you know. You could have a lover, for instance.

Tart: What makes you think I haven't got one?

Count: Yes, yes, I know — but I mean one man — one — who'd take care of you so that you wouldn't have to go with just any one.

Dirne: I geh' auch nicht mit ein' jeden. Gott sei Dank, das hab'
   i net notwendig, ich such' mir s' schon aus. [Graf sieht
   sich im Zimmer um. Dirne bemerkt das.] Im nächsten
   Monat zieh'n wir in die Stadt, in die Spiegelgasse.
Graf: Wir? Wer denn?
Dirne: Na, die Frau, und die paar anderen Mädeln, die noch
   da wohnen.
Graf: Da wohnen noch solche —
Dirne: Da daneben .... hörst net .... das ist die Milli, die auch
   im Kaffeehaus g'wesen ist.
Graf: Da schnarcht wer.
Dirne: Das ist schon die Milli, die schnarcht jetzt weiter 'n
   ganzen Tag bis um zehn auf d' Nacht. Dann steht s' auf
   und geht ins Kaffeehaus.
Graf: Das ist doch ein schauderhaftes Leben.
Dirne: Freilich. Die Frau gift' sich auch genug. Ich bin schon
   um zwölfe Mittag immer auf der Gassen.
Graf: Was machst denn um zwölf auf der Gassen?
Dirne: Was werd' ich denn machen? Auf den Strich geh' ich
   halt.
Graf: Ah so .... natürlich .... [Steht auf, nimmt die Brieftasche
   heraus, legt ihr eine Banknote auf das Nachtkastel.]
   Adieu!
Dirne: Gehst schon .... Servus .... Komm bald wieder. [Legt
   sich auf die Seite.]
Graf: [bleibt wieder stehen.] Du, sag' einmal, dir ist schon
   alles egal — was?
Dirne: Was?
Graf: Ich mein', dir macht's gar keine Freud' mehr.
Dirne: [gähnt.] Ein' Schlaf hab' ich.
Graf: Dir ist alles eins ob einer jung ist oder alt oder ob einer
   ....
Dirne: Was fragst denn?
Graf: .... Also [plötzlich auf etwas kommend.] meiner Seel',
   jetzt weiß ich, an wen du mich erinnerst, das ist ....
Dirne: Schau i wem gleich?
Graf: Unglaublich, unglaublich, jetzt bitt' ich dich aber sehr,
   red' gar nichts, eine Minute wenigstens ... [schaut sie

Tart: I don't go with just any one. Thank God I don't have to, I pick 'em out alright! [Count looks around the room. She notices it.] Next month we're moving downtown, where it's sweller.

Count: We? Who's we?

Tart: Well, the Madam and the other girls who live here.

Count: There are still others here —?

Tart: Right next door ... don't you hear? ... that's Milly, she was in the Café too.

Count: Somebody's snoring there.

Tart: That's Milly, alright, she snores all day till ten at night, an' then she gets up and goes to the Café.

Count: But that's a horrible life.

Tart: Sure it is. It makes the Madam sore, too. I'm always on the street by twelve noon, myself.

Count: What do you do on the street at twelve?

Tart: What do you think I do? Work my beat.

Count: Oh yes ... of course ... [Stands up, takes out his wallet, puts a bill on her night-table.] Goodbye!

Tart: Going already? ... So long ... Come back soon. [Turns on her side.]

Count: [Stops again.] Tell me ... I suppose everything's about the same to you, isn't it?

Tart: What?

Count: I mean, you don't get any pleasure out of it any more, do you?

Tart: [Yawning.] God, I'm sleepy.

Count: It's all the same to you whether a man's young or old, whether he ...

Tart: What are you talking about?

Count: Well ... [Suddenly struck by something.] 'Pon my soul, now I know whom you remind me of, it's ...

Tart: Do I look like somebody?

Count: Unbelievable, unbelievable, but please, just for a minute, don't speak at all, please ... [Looks at her.]

an.] ganz dasselbe G'sicht, ganz dasselbe G'sicht. [Er küßt sie plötzlich auf die Augen.]

Dirne: Na ....

Graf: Meiner Seel', es ist schad', daß du .... nichts and'res bist .... Du könnt'st ja dein Glück machen!

Dirne: Du bist g'rad wie der Franz.

Graf: Wer ist Franz?

Dirne: Na der Kellner von unser'm Kaffeehaus ....

Graf: Wieso bin ich grad' so wie der Franz?

Dirne: Der sagt auch alleweil, ich könnt' mein Glück machen und ich soll ihn heiraten.

Graf: Warum tust du's nicht?

Dirne: Ich dank' schön .... ich möcht' nicht heiraten, nein, um keinen Preis. Später einmal vielleicht.

Graf: Die Augen .... ganz die Augen ... Der Lulu möcht' sicher sagen, ich bin ein Narr — aber ich will dir noch einmal die Augen küssen .... so .... und jetzt grüß dich Gott, jetzt geh' ich.

Dirne: Servus ....

Graf: [bei der Thür.] Du ... sag' ... wundert dich das gar nicht ...

Dirne: Was denn?

Graf: Daß ich nichts von dir will.

Dirne: Es gibt viel Männer, die in der Früh nicht aufgelegt sind.

Graf: Na ja ... [Für sich.] Zu dumm, daß ich will, sie soll sich wundern ... Also Servus ... [Er ist bei der Thür.] Eigentlich ärger' ich mich. Ich weiß doch, daß es solchen Frauenzimmern nur aufs Geld ankommt ... was sag' ich — solchen ... es ist schön ... daß sie sich wenigstens nicht verstellt, das sollte einen eher freuen ... Du — weißt, ich komm nächstens wieder zu dir.

Dirne: [mit geschlossenen Augen.] Gut.

Graf: Wann bist du immer zu Haus?

Dirne: Ich bin immer zu Haus. Brauchst nur nach der Leocadia zu fragen.

Graf: Leokadia .... Schön — Also grüß dich Gott. [Bei der Thür.] Ich hab' doch noch immer den Wein im Kopf.

Exactly the same face, exactly the same face. [Kisses her suddenly on the eyes.]

Tart: Well ...

Count: 'Pon my soul, it's too bad that you're ... nothing but a ... You could make your fortune!

Tart: You're just like Franz.

Count: Who's Franz?

Tart: He's the waiter at our Café ...

Count: How am I just like Franz?

Tart: He's always saying I could make my fortune, too, and that I oughta marry him.

Count: Why don't you?

Tart: Thank you for nothing! ... I don't want to marry, not on your life, not for no price. Maybe later on.

Count: The eyes ... the identical eyes ... Louis would most certainly call me an idiot, but I must kiss your eyes once more ... there ... and now, so long, I'm off.

Tart: So long ...

Count: [At the door.] By the way ... aren't you at all surprised that ...

Tart: That what?

Count: That I don't want anything from you?

Tart: Lots of men don't feel like it in the morning.

Count: Oh well ... [To himself.] stupid of me to expect her to feel surprised ... Well, so long ... [Stands at the door.] It's really very annoying, all this. I know perfectly well that it's only a question of money to women like that ... but why say "women like that" ... at least she makes no bones about it, that's something to be thankful for ... Say ... I'll be in to see you soon.

Tart: [With her eyes closed.] Good.

Count: When are you likely to be at home?

Tart: I'm always home. All you got to do is ask for Leocadia.

Count: Leocadia ... Fine ... Well, good luck to you. [At the door.] The wine's still got me. Really, that beats

Also das ist doch das Höchste ... ich bin bei so einer und
hab' nichts getan, als ihr die Augen geküßt, weil sie
mich an wen erinnert hat ... [Wendet sich zu ihr.] Du,
Leokadie, passiert dir das öfter, daß man so weggeht
von dir?

Dirne: Wie denn?

Graf: So wie ich?

Dirne: In der Früh?

Graf: Nein .... ob schon manchmal wer bei dir war, — und
nichts von dir wollen hat?

Dirne: Nein, das ist mir noch nie g'scheh'n.

Graf: Also, was meinst denn? Glaubst, du g'fallst mir nicht?

Dirne: Warum soll ich dir denn nicht g'fallen? Bei der Nacht
hab' ich dir schon g'fallen.

Graf: Du g'fallst mir auch jetzt.

Dirne: Aber bei der Nacht hab' ich dir besser g'fallen.

Graf: Warum glaubst du das?

Dirne: Na, was fragst denn so dumm?

Graf: Bei der Nacht ... ja, sag', bin ich denn nicht gleich am
Divan hing'fallen?

Dirne: Na freilich ... mit mir zusammen.

Graf: Mit dir?

Dirne: Ja, weißt denn du das nimmer?

Graf: Ich hab' ..... wir sind zusammen ...... ja ....

Dirne: Aber gleich bist eing'schlafen.

Graf: Gleich bin ich ... So ... Also so war das!...

Dirne: Ja, Bubi. Du mußt aber ein' ordentlichen Rausch
g'habt haben, daß dich nimmer erinnerst.

Graf: So ... — Und doch .... es ist eine entfernte Ähnlichkeit ...
Servus ... [Lauscht.] Was ist denn los?

Dirne: Das Stubenmäd'l ist schon auf. Geh', gib ihr was
beim Hinausgeh'n. Das Tor ist auch offen, ersparst den
Hausmeister.

Graf: Ja. [Im Vorzimmer.] Also ... Es wär' doch schön
gewesen, wenn ich sie nur auf die Augen geküßt hätt'.
Das wäre beinahe ein Abenteuer gewesen ... Es war mir
halt nicht bestimmt. [Das Stubenmädel steht da, öffnet
die Thür.] Ah — da haben S' ... Gute Nacht. —

everything ... I come to a female like this and don't do anything but kiss her eyes, because she reminds me of somebody ... [Turns to her.] Tell me, Leocadia, does that happen to you often, a man going away like this?

Tart: Like what?

Count: The way I'm going ...

Tart: Early, you mean?

Count: No ... I mean, men being with you — and not wanting anything from you?

Tart: No, it's never happened to me before.

Count: Well, what do you make of it? Do you think I don't like you?

Tart: Why shouldn't you like me? You liked me good enough last night.

Count: I like you now too.

Tart: But you liked me better in the night?

Count: What makes you think that?

Tart: What a silly thing to ask!

Count: Last night ... but see here, didn't I tumble right onto the sofa?

Tart: Sure ... we both did, together.

Count: Together?

Tart: Yes, don't you remember?

Count: I ... we were ... yes ...

Tart: But you went to sleep right off.

Count: Right off ... I see ... so that was it!

Tart: Yes, sonny. You must have been good and pickled not to remember that.

Count: I see ... and yet ... there is a remote resemblance ... So long ... [Listens.] What's that noise?

Tart: The maid's up already. You might give her something when you go out. The street door is open, too, so that'll save you the janitor's tip.

Count: Yes. [In the hall.] Well ... it would have been beautiful if I'd only kissed her eyes. That would have been an adventure, almost ... but I guess it wasn't to be ... [The maid opens the door, stands there.] Ah — here, take this ... Good night.

Stubenmädchen: Guten Morgen.
Graf: Ja freilich ... guten Morgen ... guten Morgen.

ENDE

Maid: Good morning.
Count: Oh yes, of course ... Good morning ... good morning.

THE END

CPSIA information can be obtained
at www.ICGtesting.com
Printed in the USA
LVHW031501181118
597559LV00001B/70/P